ALL THE
LAW YOU SHOULD KNOW

Jeremy Farley

Emerald Guides

ISBN
978-1-84716-643-2

Printed by 4edge www.4edge.co.uk

Cover design by Straightforward Graphics

CONTENTS

INTRODUCTION

We are all bound by the law and the British legal system. The framework of the law affects us in many ways, directly and indirectly. Right throughout our lives we will need to have a basic knowledge of the law. In this way, we can operate as citizens more effectively and we can also have a greater understanding of our rights and obligations.

The book is not a detailed textbook on the law. The purpose is to outline the law, in enough depth, and ensuring that the reader has understood the law and can then apply that law in a practical way.

This book covers, in the main, the legal system as it operates in England and Wales. To cover Scottish law in the same book would have been too great a task.

This edition has been revised in the light of the referendum result and the UK voting to leave the EU. However, all references to EU law throughout the book are still relevant until such time as we leave.

An attempt has been made to outline the operation of the legal system and also to describe the players in that system, such as solicitors and barristers and to describe the framework of financial aid that can be accessed through the legal help scheme. There is a detailed chapter on putting together a small claim and going to court with that claim. For many people, the small claims court is the most common method of seeking redress against an individual or company.

The chapters that follow the small claims court cover accidents and compensation, law and the consumer, legal relationship between children and adults, financial provisions for children, divorce, bereavement and the law, producing a will, the law and neighbours, landlord and tenant and, finally, the law and the police, what to do if you are arrested and how to complain.

The more complicated our society becomes, the more it becomes controlled by laws and regulations, the more that the individual needs to know to be able to be effective. This book cannot hope to be totally comprehensive but does cover as many key areas as possible.

Ch. 1

Understanding the Legal System-How it Works

Legal terms explained

There is a glossary of terms at the back of this book which deals with commonly used legal jargon. However, it is useful to highlight the most common terms right at the outset, as they will be used frequently throughout the book:

Claimant – when legal proceedings are brought, the person or persons, or organisation, bringing the case is called the claimant.

Defendant – The individual or organisation being sued, and therefore defending, is called the defendant.

Solicitor – a solicitor is the lawyer you will see for legal advice relating to your case. This person will have undertaken many years of study and passed all the necessary legal examinations. We will be discussing solicitors in more depth a little later.

Barrister – A Barrister is a lawyer who is a specialist in what is known as advocacy, i.e. speaking in court. A Barrister will have been called to the bar by one of the Inns of Court and passed the barristers professional examinations. A solicitor will instruct a barrister to represent you in court proceedings. However, barristers will not normally be the persons giving individuals legal advice in the first instance. The legal profession is, basically, split into two, barristers and solicitors, both of whom are lawyers.

Writ – A judicial writ is issued to bring legal proceedings. Civil cases are started in the courts by issuing and serving a writ. This document is completed either by an individual bringing the case or by a solicitor on behalf of the individual. It is issued by the court.

Litigant in person – a litigant is someone who is bringing legal proceedings or suing. A litigant-in-person is someone who chooses to represent themselves in court, without a lawyer.

Damages – Civil claims in the courts are for damages, which is money claimed from the defendant to compensate the claimant for loss arising from the action of default of the defendant. An example might be the sale of a good that has caused injury to a person and it is alleged that the good was faulty at the time of purchase.

Using the legal system to resolve disputes

If you are contemplating any form of legal action, with or without solicitors, it is necessary to have a basic idea of how the system works. The more that you understand the processes underlying the legal system, the more effective you will be, both as a citizen and as a potential litigant.

The structure of the court system

The court system in the United Kingdom deals, in the main, with civil and criminal cases. They are heard in either the county court (civil cases) and the Magistrates and Crown Courts (criminal cases).

Civil cases are those that typically involve breaches of contract, personal injury claims, divorce cases, bankruptcy hearings, debt problems, some employment cases, landlord and tenant disputes and other consumer disputes, such as faulty goods.

Criminal cases are those such as offences against the person, theft, damage to property, murder and fraud. These cases, if of a non-serious nature, are heard in the magistrate's courts. If of a serious nature, then they will be heard in the Crown Court and tried by jury.

Criminal cases

The more serious criminal cases are tried on the basis of a document called the *indictment.* The defendant is indicted on criminal charges specified in the indictment by the prosecutor. In most cases, the prosecution is on behalf of the Crown (State) and is handled by an official agency called the Crown Prosecution Service, which takes the case over from the police who have already investigated most of the evidence. The first stage will be to decide whether there is a case to answer. This process, called committal, will be dealt with by a magistrate on the basis of evidence disclosed in papers provided by the prosecutor. If the case proceeds, it is heard in the Crown Court. There are about 70 Branches of the Crown Court in the United Kingdom. The trial is before a judge and jury. The judge presides over the trial and considers legal issues. The jury will decide on the facts (who is telling the truth) and applies the law to those facts. In criminal cases, the prosecution has to prove, beyond reasonable doubt, that the defendant is guilty. The defendant does not have to prove innocence. However, it is the jury who will observe the prosecutor and defending lawyer and decide the case.

In less serious criminal cases (which comprise over 90% of criminal cases) the case is sent for summary and trial in one of over 400 *magistrates* courts. A summary trial means that there is no committal or jury. The case is decided by a bench of magistrates. In most cases there are three magistrates who are lay (unqualified) persons but are from the local community. However, there are now an increasing number of 'stipendiary' magistrates, paid magistrates who are qualified lawyers.

Those defendants in criminal cases who are dissatisfied with verdicts may be able to appeal, as follows:

- from the Magistrates courts there is an appeal to the Crown Court on matters of fact or law.
- From the Crown Court, it might be possible to appeal to the Criminal Division of the court of Appeal on matters of fact or law.
- Certain legal disputes arising in the Magistrates court or the Crown Court can be taken before the divisional court of the High Court.

- Matters of important legal dispute arising in the Crown Court can be taken to the Supreme Court.

Civil cases

The majority of people who buy this book will be taking civil action of one form or another. Increasingly, people are becoming litigants-in-person as this enables people to access the courts and obtain justice without incurring high costs. The only real costs are the court fees and other incidental costs such as taking time off work and so on.

The county court

The county court deals with civil cases, which are dealt with by a judge, or a district judge. A case can be started in any county court but can be transferred back to the defendant's local court.

All cases arising from regulated credit agreements must be started in the county court, whatever their value.

County courts deal with a wide range of cases ranging from bankruptcy and family matters to landlord and tenant disputes. The most common cases are:

- Consumer disputes, for example faulty goods or services
- Personal injury claims, caused by negligence, for example traffic accidents, accidents caused by faulty pavements and roads, potholes etc
- Debt problems, for example someone seeking payment Some undefended divorce cases and some domestic violence cases
- Race and sex discrimination cases
- Employment problems, usually involving pay.

Small claims in the county court

A case in the county court, if it is defended, is dealt with in one of three ways. These ways are called 'tracks' The court will, when considering a case, decide which procedure to apply and allocate the case to one of the following tracks:

- The small claims track

- The fast track
- The multi-track

The small claims track is the most commonly used and is the track for claims of £5000 or less. Overall, the procedure in the small claims track is simpler than the other tracks and costs are not usually paid by the losing party.

Following a brief summary of the other courts in the United Kingdom, we will be looking in more detail, in chapter 4, at how to commence and process a small claim. In the main, readers of this book will be concerned with the small claims track and it is therefore necessary to outline that process in depth. We will also be looking, in chapter 2, at the legal help scheme. This scheme enables those with a low income to get free legal advice from a solicitor and assistance with preparing a case.

The magistrates' court

As we have seen, magistrate's courts deal with criminal cases in the first instance and also deal with some civil cases.

The cases are heard by Justices of the Peace or by District Judges (magistrates courts). All cases heard in a magistrate's court are from within their own area.

Criminal offences in the magistrate's court

Magistrate's courts deal with criminal offences where the defendant is not entitled to a trial by jury. These are known as 'summary offences' and involve a maximum penalty of six months imprisonment and/or a fine up to £5000. Magistrates also deal with offences where the defendant can choose trial by jury. If this is the case, the case is passed up to the Crown Court.

The youth court

The youth court deals with young people who have committed criminal offences, and who are aged between 10-17. The youth court is a part of the magistrate's court and up to three specially trained magistrates hear the case. If a young person is charged with a very serious offence, which in the case of an adult is punishable by 14 years imprisonment or more, the youth court can commit him/her for trial at the Crown Court.

Civil cases in the magistrates' court

As we have seen, the vast majority of civil cases are dealt with in the county courts. However, the magistrate's court can deal with a limited number of cases, as follows:

- Some civil debts, e.g. arrears of income tax, national insurance contributions, council tax and Value added Tax arrears
- Licences, for example, licences for clubs and pubs
- Some matrimonial problems, e.g. maintenance payments and removing a spouse from the matrimonial home
- Welfare of children, e.g. local authority care orders or supervision orders, adoption proceedings and residence orders

The Crown Court

The more serious criminal cases are tried in the Crown Court. The following are dealt with:

- Serious criminal offences to be heard by judge and jury
- Appeals from the magistrates court-which are dealt with by a judge and at least two magistrates
- Someone convicted in the magistrates court may be referred to the Crown Court for sentencing.

The High Court

The High Court will hear appeals in criminal cases and will also deal with certain civil cases. The High Court also has the legal power to review the actions or activities of individuals and organisations to make sure that they are both operating within the law and also are acting justly. The High Court consists of three divisions, as follows:

The Family Division

The Family Division of the High Court will deal with more complex defended divorce cases, wardship, adoption, domestic violence and other cases. It will also deal with appeals from the magistrates and county courts in matrimonial cases.

The Queens Bench Division

The Queens Bench Division of the High Court will deal with larger claims for compensation, and also more complex cases for compensation. A limited number of appeals from county and magistrates courts are also dealt with. The Queens Bench Division can also review the actions of individuals or organisations and hear libel and slander cases.

The Chancery Division

The Chancery Division deals with trusts, contested wills, winding up companies, bankruptcy, mortgages, charities, and contested revenue such as income tax.

The Court of Appeal

The Court of Appeal deals with civil and criminal appeals. Civil appeals from the high and county courts are heard, as well as from the Employment Appeals Tribunal and the Lands Tribunal. Criminal Appeals include appeals against convictions in the Crown Courts, and points of law referred by the Attorney General following acquittal in the Crown Court or where a sentence imposed is seen as too lenient.

The Supreme Court

The Supreme Court deals mostly with appeals from the Court of Appeal, where the case involves a point of law of public importance. Appeals are mostly about civil cases although the Lords do deal with some criminal appeals. If there is dissatisfaction with a finding of the Supreme Court the claimant can take a case higher through the European Court System.

The Court of First Instance

The Court of First Instance is based in Luxembourg. A case can be taken to this court if European Community law has not been implemented properly by a national government or there is confusion over its interpretation or it has been ignored. A case which is lost in the Court of First Instance may be taken to appeal to the European Court of Justice.

The European Court of Justice of the European Communities

The European Court of Justice advises on interpretation of European Community law and takes action against infringements. It examines whether the actions of those members of the European Community are valid and clarifies European Community law by making preliminary rulings. It also hears appeals against decisions made by the Court of First Instance.

The European Court of Human Rights

The European Court of Human Rights deals with cases in which a person thinks that their human rights have been contravened and for which there is no legal remedy within the national legal system.

****

Ch. 2

The Legal Profession

In the English Legal System, there are two types of lawyers, Barristers and Solicitors. The Law Society oversees the activities of solicitors as well as the legal profession as a whole. The General Council of the Bar oversees Barristers.

Solicitors

To become a solicitor it is usual to either have a law degree or have completed an extra year of law if the degree is a non-law degree. This is called the Common Professional Examination.

When the course has been completed successfully the student is still not a solicitor. A training contract must be obtained from a firm of solicitors and two years work must be completed. This training period can also be undertaken in other legal organisations such as the Crown Prosecution Service, or the legal department of a local authority. During the training period he or she will have to undertake their own work and complete a 20 day Professional Skills Course after which time the person will be admitted as a solicitor by the Law Society. Even after qualifying, solicitors have to attend continuing education to keep their skills up to date.

There is a non-graduate route to become a solicitor for mature candidates but the process takes longer to complete.

Solicitors who qualify will either work in private practice in a solicitors firm, or can work for the Crown Prosecution Service or for a local authority or government department. Some will become legal advisors to big companies.

Solicitors will work in sole practices or partnerships and the type of work carried out will be varied depending largely on the specialism of the firm. A small firm will usually cover a whole range of matters from housing, family, conveyancing and business matters. It is usual for a solicitor to specialise in a particular area.

All solicitors can act as advocates in the Magistrates Court. After 1986 solicitors can appear in a High Court to make a statement after a case has been settled.

Complaints against solicitors

A client can sue a solicitor for negligence in and out of court work. One case where this happened was Griffiths v Dawson (1993) where solicitors for the plaintiff failed to make a correct application in divorce proceedings against her husband. As a result of this the plaintiff lost financially and the solicitors were ordered to pay £21,000 compensation.

Solicitors Regulation Society

The Solicitors Regulation Society deals with complaints against solicitors. It is funded by the Law Society.

Barristers

Collectively, barristers are referred to as 'the Bar' and they are controlled by their own professional body-the General Council of the Bar. All barristers must also be a member of one of the four Inns of Court, Lincolns Inn, Inner Temple, Middle Temple and Gray's Inn all of which are situated near the Royal Courts of Justice in London.

Entry to the Bar is usually degree based although a small number of mature entrants can qualify. As with solicitor's graduates with a non-law degree can take a one-year course for the Common Professional Examination in the core subjects in order to qualify as a barrister. All student barristers must pass the Bar Vocational Course which emphasises the practical skills of drafting pleadings for use in court negotiation and advocacy.

All student barristers must join one of the four Inns of Court. Until 1997 it was mandatory to dine there 12 times before being called to the Bar. However, students may now attend in a different way, such as a weekend residential course.

After being called to the Bar a Barrister must complete a practical stage of the training called pupillage. This is on-the-job training where the trainee barrister becomes a pupil to a qualified barrister. This involves shadowing the barrister and can be with the same barrister for 12 months or with two barristers for six months each. There is also a requirement to take part in ongoing continuing education organised by the Bar Council. After the first six months of pupillage barristers can appear on their own in court.

Barristers practicing at the Bar are self-employed but share the administrative expenses of a set of chambers. Most sets of chambers comprise 15-29 barristers. They will employ a clerk as an administrator. The majority of barristers will concentrate on advocacy, although there are some who will specialise.

Originally, it was necessary for anyone who wanted to instruct a barrister to go to a solicitor first. The solicitor would then brief the barrister. After September 2004, it has been possible for anyone to contact barristers direct. However, direct access is still not allowed for criminal work or family work.

Barristers can be employed direct (the employed bar) working for example, for the Crown Prosecution Service and can represent in court.

Queen's Counsel

After a Barrister or solicitor has served at least 16 years with an advocacy qualification, it is then possible to become a Queens Counsel (QC). About 10% of the Bar are Queens Counsel and it is known as 'taking silk'. QC's usually take on complicated, high profile cases. Until 2004 Queen's Counsel were appointed by the Lord Chancellor. After 2004, selection is by a panel chaired by a non-lawyer. Selection is by interview and applicants can provide references.

Complaints against barristers

Where a barrister receives a brief from a solicitor he or she does not enter into a contract with a client and so cannot sue if fees are not paid.

Likewise the client cannot sue for breach of contract. However, they can be sued for negligence. In the case Saif Ali v Sydney Mitchell and Co (1990) it was held that a barrister could be sued for negligence in respect of written advice and opinions. In that particular case a barrister had given wrong advice on who to sue, with the result that the claimant was too late to start proceedings against the right person.

Solicitors and barristers summarised

	Solicitors	Barristers
Professional body	Law Society	Bar Council
Basic qualifications	Law degree or non-law degree with one years Common Professional Exam	Law degree or non-law degree with one years Common Professional Exam
Vocational training	Legal practice course	Bar vocational course
Practical training	Training contract	Pupillage
Methods of working	Firm of partners or sole practitioner	Self-employed Practicing in Chambers
Rights of audience	Normally only County Court and Magistrates Court	All courts
Relationship with client	Contractual	Normally through solicitor but Accountants and Surveyors can Brief barristers Directly
Liability	Liable in contract and tort to clients may also be liable to others affected by negligence	No contractual liability but liable for negligence

The Judiciary

Collectively, judges are known as the judiciary. The head of the Judiciary is the Lord Chancellor.

Types of judges

Superior judges

Superior judges are those in the high court and above. These are (from top to bottom):

- The 12 justices of the Supreme Court
- The Lords Justices of Appeal in the Court of Appeal
- Master of the Rolls (Court of Appeal Civil Division)
- Lord Justice of Appeal-Court of Appeal
- High Court Judges (known as puisne judges) who sit in the three divisions of the High Court

Specific posts heading the different divisions of the Court of Appeal and the High Court are:

- The Lord Chief Justice, who is the president of the Criminal Division of the Court of Appeal and the senior judge in the Queens Bench Division of the High Court
- The Master of the Rolls who is president of the Civil Division of the Court of Appeal
- The President of the Family Division of the High Court
- The Vice Chancellor of the Chancery Division of the High Court

Inferior judges

The inferior judges are:

- Circuit judges who sit in both the Crown Court and the County Court
- Recorders who are part-time judges sitting usually in the Crown Court though some may be assigned to the County Court
- District judges who hear small claims and other matters in the County Court
- District judges (Magistrates Court) who sit in Magistrates Courts in the major towns and cities

To become a judge at any level it is necessary to have qualified as a barrister or solicitor. It is not essential to have practiced, as the Courts and Legal Services Act 1990 provided for academic lawyers to be appointed.

Lords Justices of Appeal

Lords Justices of Appeal must have a 10-year High Court Qualification or be an existing High Court Judge.

High Court Judges

To be eligible to be a High Court Judge it is necessary either to have had the right to practice in the High Court for 10 years or more or to have been a Circuit Judge for at least 2 years. New qualifications give solicitors the chance to become High Court Judges. It is also possible for academic lawyers who have not practiced as barristers or solicitors to be appointed.

Circuit judges

To become a circuit judge a candidate can either have had rights of audience for 10 years or more in either the Crown Court or County Court or to have been a recorder. The Courts and Legal Services Act 1990 also allows for promotion after being a district judge, stipendiary magistrate or chairman of an employment tribunal for at least three years.

Recorders

A Recorder is a part-time post. The applicant must have practiced as a barrister or solicitor for at least 10 years.

District judges

District judges need a seven-year general qualification. They are appointed from either barristers or solicitors. District judges in the Magistrates Court need the same qualification.

Law Officers

There is a law office within government that advises on matters of law that affects government. There are two law officers: the Attorney General and the Solicitor General. Both are members of the government of the day and are appointed by the Prime Minister. Both will usually be Members of the House of Commons. The Attorney General appoints the Director of Public Prosecutions, who heads the Crown Prosecution Service.

The Attorney General

The Attorney General is the Government's chief legal advisor. He is not a member of the main cabinet. He will advise government on legislative proposals and on criminal proceedings which have a political or public element. He is also responsible for major litigation which involves the government.

The Attorney General is appointed from those members of Parliament who are barristers and he can represent the government in court proceedings. He is the head of the English Bar but cannot practice privately as a barrister.

The Attorney General's consent is required before a prosecution can commence in certain cases such as corruption, possessing explosive substances and hijacking. He can grant immunity from prosecution and can stop proceedings for an indictable offence. He can also instruct the Director of Public Prosecutions to take over any private prosecution.

The Attorney General has the right to refer any criminal cases to the Court of Appeal (Criminal Division) for a point of law to be considered following an acquittal in the Crown Court and he can appeal against a sentence which is considered too lenient.

The Solicitor General

The Solicitor General acts as a deputy to the Attorney General.

The Director of Public Prosecutions

The DPP's duties are set out in the Prosecution of Offences Act 1985, which created the Crown Prosecution Service. The DPP must be a barrister or solicitor of at least 10 years standing. The appointment is made by the Attorney General to whom the DPP is accountable. The main function of the DPP is to head the Crown Prosecution Service. The other functions are set out in the Prosecution of Offences Act 1985, which are:

- To take over the conduct of all criminal proceedings instituted by the police
- To institute and oversee the conduct of criminal proceedings where the importance of difficulty of the proceedings makes this appropriate
- To take over the conduct of binding over proceedings brought by the police
- To give advice to police forces on all matters relating to criminal offences
- To appear for the prosecution in certain appeals

Magistrates
Lay magistrates

Lay magistrates, otherwise known as Justices of the Peace sit to hear cases as a bench of two or three magistrates. Single magistrates can issue search warrants and warrants for arrest.

Lay magistrates do not have to have any qualifications in law. They must, however, be suitable in character and integrity and also have an understanding of the work that they perform. There are formal requirements as to age and residence and a magistrate must live within the area where they will sit: lay magistrates must be aged between 18 and 65 on appointment.

Some people are not eligible to be appointed, including people with a serious criminal record, though minor offences such as driving offences will not disqualify a person. Others who are disqualified are undischarged bankrupts, members of the forces and those whose work is not compatible with sitting as a magistrate, such as police officers. About 1,500 new lay magistrates are appointed each year, by the Lord Chancellor.

Duties of magistrates

Magistrates have a wide workload mainly connected to criminal cases, although they also deal with civil matters. The criminal cases involve early administrative hearings, remand hearings, bail applications and committal proceedings. They also deal with debt related civil matters such as non-payment of utility bills, council tax etc. In addition, they will also hear appeals relating to the refusal of the local authority to grant licences for the sale of alcohol and for betting and gaming establishments.

Specially trained justices will form the Youth Court to hear criminal charges against young offenders aged from 10-17years old. There is also a special panel to hear cases including orders for protection against violence, affiliation cases, adoption orders and proceedings under the Children Act 1989.

Lay magistrates also sit at the Crown Court to hear appeals from the Magistrates Court. In these cases the lay justices form a panel with a qualified judge.

The Magistrate's clerk

Every bench of magistrates is assisted by a clerk. The senior clerk in each court has to be qualified as a barrister or solicitor for at least five years. The clerk's duty is to advise the magistrates on questions of law, practice and procedure. The Crime and Disorder Act 1998 also gives clerks the powers to deal with Early Administrative Hearings.

****

3

Legal Aid and Advice

Many people will require legal assistance of one sort or another when either taking or defending a legal action. Lack of knowledge and difficulty in meeting costs are the two main reasons for needing assistance.

One principal issue for the provision of legal services (both civil and criminal) is the quantum of public funding-as the Justice Secretary explained on 30th June 2010:

'Our legal aid system has grown to an extent that we spend more than almost anywhere else in the world. France spends £3 per head of the population, Germany £5, New Zealand £8. In England and Wales, we spend a staggering £38 per head of population.

Anther principal issue is the nature of services provided (advice, professional, representation or both) in respect of criminal and civil law.

The Legal Aid Agency
The Legal Aid Agency provides both civil and criminal legal aid and advice in England and Wales.

The work of the LAA is essential to the fair, effective and efficient operation of the civil and criminal justice systems. They are a delivery organisation which commissions and procures legal aid services from providers (solicitors, barristers and the not-for-profit sector).

Governance
The Legal Aid Agency is an executive agency of the Ministry of Justice. It came into existence on 1 April 2013 following the abolition of the Legal Services Commission as a result of the Legal Aid, Sentencing and Punishment of Offenders (LASPO) Act 2012.

The Act created the new statutory office of the Director of Legal Casework. The Director will take decisions on the funding of individual cases. Processes have been put in place to ensure the Legal Aid Agency is able to demonstrate independence of decision-making. There will be an annual report published about these decisions.

Strategic objectives
The priorities of the LAA are to:

- improve casework to reduce cost, enhance control and give better customer service
- improve organisational capability to meet the challenges ahead, including developing and engaging our people
- build and maintain strong partnerships to secure quality provision and contribute fully to wider justice and Government aims

Other parts of the organisation

Public Defender Service

The Public Defender Service (PDS) is a department of the Legal Aid Agency that operates alongside private providers delivering a full range of quality services within the criminal defence market from advice and representation at the police station and magistrates courts through to advocacy in the higher courts.

Legal Aid and financial help
Legal Aid, (previously known as Public Funding) allows for state funding of legal cases in certain very limited legal and financial circumstances.

As mentioned above, Legal Aid has changed due to the Legal Aid, Sentencing and Punishment of Offenders Act 2012, which came into force on 1st April 2013.

Applicants for legal aid must show that they meet the financial test and that their case has a reasonable prospect of being successful. There must also be no alternative sources of funding or representation available that would be more suitable for your case.

Due to the changes in legal aid the type of cases that could potentially be funded through legal aid has been reduced. The following is a list of case areas that can still potentially be funded:

Clinical Negligence
Only for children with neurological injury suffered during pregnancy, birth or postnatal period of 8 weeks, which results in severe disability.

Debt

- Repossession of your home by mortgage lender
- Orders for sale of your home
- Involuntary bankruptcy, if includes your home, (includes statutory demand)

Discrimination
Where the Equality Act 2010 has been breached. This is where a person has been discriminated against for one or more of the following - age, race, disability, religion, sex, sexual orientation, gender reassignment, marriage or civil partnership, pregnancy or maternity.

Education (special educational needs)
Special education needs under the Education Act 1996, and assessments relating to learning difficulties under the Learning and Skills Act 2000.

Family
- Public family law relating to the protection of children
- Family cases where evidence of domestic violence

- Children cases where evidence of child abuse
- Child abduction matters
- The representation of children in private family cases
- Legal advice as part of mediation
- Domestic violence injunction cases
- Forced marriage protection order cases

Housing

- Repossession of your home, (other than by a mortgage lender)
- Eviction from your home, both lawful and unlawful eviction
- Repairs to rented property where condition of property poses serious threat to your health or safety
- Homelessness, where you are homeless or risk being made homeless
- Injunctions under the Protection from Harassment Act 1997 in housing matters

Immigration & Asylum

- Where you are seeking asylum
- Domestic violence injunctions
- Special Immigration Appeals Commission (SIAC) proceedings
- Leave to enter or remain in the UK for victims of human trafficking

Mediation

Mediation in family law cases, to reach an agreement without having to go to court.

Welfare Benefits

- Appeals on a point of law to the Upper Tribunal
- Appeals on a point of law to the Court of Appeal and Supreme Court

Other Areas

Mental health, community care, actions against public authorities and public law cases.

There are other various forms of help, such as legal help and criminal public funding. Criminal public funding is not means tested, and so is available to everyone.

If your case is publicly funded and you win compensation or damages or hang onto to your property or assets a statutory charge will be applied. This is to recover the legal costs incurred in your case.

Law centres

Law centres offer a free non-means tested legal service to people in their area. Funding has always been a problem for law centres and many are reliant on grants. As a result many have closed. Those which have remained open will deal with the needs of the community they serve, undertaking work such as housing, planning, the environment, employment, immigration and consumer matters. The list is not exhaustive.

The Criminal Defence Service

Under s 12 of the Access to Justice act 1999, The Legal services Commission established a Legal Defence Service. This service is aimed at 'securing that individuals involved in criminal investigations or proceedings have access to such advice, assistance or representation as the interests of justice require'. The following schemes are offered:

Duty Solicitors

Section 13 of the Access to Justice Act 1999 states that the Commission shall fund advice and assistance as it considers appropriate for individuals who are arrested and held in custody. However, solicitors can no longer attend at a police station, unless the client is vulnerable, where the client is detained for:

- a non-imprisonable offence
- on a warrant
- in breach of bail conditions
- for drink drive offences.

Advice and assistance

This is limited to several hours work and can only include advocacy if the solicitor has applied for a representation order which has been refused. Usually, there is a means test for advice and assistance. However, a duty solicitor at a magistrates court can see all defendants in custody free of charge under the advice and assistance scheme.

Representation

This covers the costs of a solicitor to prepare the defence before the case gets to court. It also covers representation at court, including issues such as bail. If a barrister is required then this will be covered.

****

Ch. 4

Using the Small Claims Court-Commencing a Small Claim

Having looked briefly at the operations of the legal system, it is now necessary to examine the processes involved in commencing a small claim in the county court. Although a claim depends on the subject matter, the majority of people tend to take action in the county court small claims division.

Commencing a claim

A person can start legal action in any court and if the case is defended the court will decide what procedure to use. If the case is a simple one, with a value of £5000 or less, the court will decide that the small claims procedure will be used and will allocate the case to the small claims track. In most cases, the court will not order that costs are paid by the losing party in a small claims case. For this reason, most people do not use a solicitor when making a small claim. It may, however, be possible to get legal help using the legal help scheme. In addition, it is possible to commence a claim by using 'Money Claims Online' which you can access by visiting the court service website www. justice.gov.uk.

Types of case dealt with in the small claims track

When the court is considering whether to allocate the case to a small claims track it will take into account a number of factors, but the main factor is the value of the case.

If the value of a case is £5000 or less it will generally be allocated to the small claims track. However, if it is a personal injury claim, it will be allocated to the small claims track only if the value of the claim for the personal injuries is not more than £1000. If the claimant is a tenant and is claiming against their landlord because repairs are needed to the premises and the cost of the work is £1000 or less, the case will be allocated to the small claims track.

Types of claims in the small claims court

The most common types of small claims are:

- Compensation for faulty goods, for example washing machines or other goods that go wrong
- Compensation for faulty services provided, for example by builders, garages and so on
- Disputes between landlords and tenants, for examples, rent arrears, compensation for not doing repairs
- Wages owed or money in lieu of notice

If a case proves to be too complex then a judge may refer the case to another track for a full hearing, even if below the limit for that track.

Actions before applying to court

As we saw in the previous chapter, before applying to court it is always necessary to try to solve the problem amicably, or as amicably as possible without recourse to legal action. A person who intends to commence a claim should write a 'letter before action' which should set out terms for settlement before applying to court.

For example, if a television is defective, or workmanship on a car is faulty, there is no point applying to court for compensation before contacting the garage or repair shop. Whilst this may seem obvious, there are cases where people do rush in. Always try to settle before launching court action. It will assist in the case if it does go to court.

Which court deals with a small claim

The court action can be started in any court, but the case can be transferred. If the claim is defended and the claim is for a fixed amount, the court will automatically transfer the case to a defendant's local court (if he or she is an individual not a company). In other cases, either party can ask for the case to be transferred.

Commencing a claim

The claimant commences a claim by filling in a claim form, obtainable from local county courts or legal stationers. They can also be obtained from the internet. The government court site is www.justice.gov.uk all forms can be obtained from this website as can a host of information on all legal topics.

The form is quite straightforward and asks for details of claimant and defendant and how much is owed. The form also asks for the particulars of the claim. The particulars set out full details of the claim. If there is not enough room on the form then a separate piece of paper can be used. The claimant has a right to spend a little more time on the particulars and can send them to the defendant separately, but no later than 14 days after the claim form.

The forms are designed to be user friendly and are accompanied by guidance notes to ensure that no mistakes are made.

The claimant may be entitled to claim interest on the claim and, if so, must give details of the interest claimed in the particulars of claim. In a personal injury claim the particulars of claim must include the claimants date of birth and brief details of the injuries. The claimant must attach a list of any past expenses and losses that they want to claim for and any expenses and losses that they may incur in the future.

Applying for the claim form to be issued

The claimant must ensure that two copies of the claim form reach the court where court action is to commence and a copy should be kept for records. There will be a fee to pay. Currently this depends on the amount of money to be claimed. You should check with your local county court, small claims division, for the current fees.

In some cases, the fee will be waived, for example if the claimant is receiving income support, working families tax credit, disabled persons tax credit or income based job seekers allowance. If none of these benefits are received, but financial hardship would be suffered if a fee was paid, the fee may also be waived. The court will stamp the claim form and then, in most cases, serve it on the defendant. The court will give the claimant a notice of issue.

Usually the court will serve the claim form by sending it to the defendant by first class post. The claimant will be deemed to have received it on the second day of posting. If the claimant wishes to serve the claim form his or herself then a request should be made and the court will provide the form and other forms that go with it.

If the case is not defended

If the defendant is not defending the case, then he or she may accept that they owe the money. If this is the case then he or she can pay the money directly to the claimant. If the defendant has accepted that they owe the money, but needs time to pay, they can propose an arrangement, for example that the amount owed is paid in instalments or all the money in one lump sum on a specified future date. If the claimant accepts this offer, he or she will have to return a form to the court requesting 'judgement by admission'. If the defendant does not keep to this agreement the claimant can then take enforcement action.

If the claimant does not accept this offer then he or she must give good reason and a court official will decide what a reasonable arrangement will be. The court will send both parties an order for payment. If the claimant is not happy with the order then he or she will have to write to the court giving reasons and sending a copy to the defendant. A judge will then decide what is reasonable for the defendant to pay. If the defendant does not keep to the arrangement, the claimant can take enforcement action.

If the defendant is defending the case

If the case is to be defended, the defendant has to respond to the claim within 14 days of service (this is the second day after posting). If the particulars of claim were served after the claim form the defendant must respond within 14 days of service of particulars of claim. A defence is launched by the defendant sending back the defence form, which was sent with the claim form.

If the defendant does not send a defence back within the time period then the claimant can ask for an order to be made against him or her.

The defendant can send the defence back to the court or can send the acknowledgement of service form sent with the defence form back to court and the defence form back within 14 days of this. This helps if more time is needed.

When the defence is sent to the court the court will send an allocation questionnaire to both the claimant and the defendant. This must be returned to the court no later than the date specified in it. When the claimant returns the allocation form a fee should also be sent although this can be waived on financial grounds. The court will use the information contained within the allocation questionnaire to decide which track to allocate the case to.

When the court has decided to allocate the case to the small claims track, the claimant and defendant will be sent a notice of allocation. This form will tell the parties what they have to do to prepare for the hearing. These instructions are called 'directions'. One example of directions may be that parties are told that they should send all copies of relevant documents to court, documents that they intend to use in court in the case against the other party. These are sent at least 14 days before the case begins.

There are standard directions for a number of common cases, for example, if the claim is to do with a holiday then there will be standard directions from the courts as to the evidence needed.

The day of the hearing

The notice of allocation will usually specify the time, day and date of hearing, where the hearing will take place and how much time has been allowed for it. If the claimant wants to attend the hearing but for some reason cannot, then a letter should be sent to the court requesting a different hearing date. A fee is payable and the court will only agree to this request if it is based on reasonable grounds.

A claimant can also ask the court to deal with a claim in his or her absence, A typical case might be where the costs and time to reach the court are disproportionate. If this is the case then a letter should reach the court at least seven days before the case.

In some cases, the court will not set a final hearing date. The following are alternatives used by the courts:

- The court could propose that the case is dealt with without a hearing. If both parties have no objections then the case can be decided on the papers only. If the parties do not reply by the date given then the court will usually take that silence as consent

- The court may hold a preliminary hearing. This could happen if the claim requires special directions which the judge wants to explain to the parties personally or where the judge feels that the claimant or defendant has no real prospect of succeeding and wants to sort out the claim as soon as possible to save everyone time and expense, or if the papers do not show any reasonable

33

grounds for bringing the claim. A preliminary hearing could become a final hearing where the case is decided.

Preparing a case

It is important that a case is prepared carefully – the court has to be convinced. A reasonable amount of time should be spent ensuring that all the facts are entered, all dates specified and all paperwork is available. The following points are a general guide to what preparation should be made:

- someone with low income can use the legal help scheme to cover the costs of legal advice, but not representation from a solicitor. This advice can be extremely useful and can include getting expert reports, for example on faulty goods. However, a report can only be used in court with permission of the court

- notes about the case should be set out in date order. This will help you to present your case and will make sense to a judge. All backing documentation should be taken to court and be presented if asked for. This documentation should be organised around the presentation, in chronological order

- damaged or faulty goods should be taken as evidence. If it is not possible to do this then photographs should be taken instead

- evidence of expenses should be taken along and any receipts kept

- all letters about the case should be taken to court

- in most cases, the claimant and defendant may be the only witnesses. If the court has agreed that other witnesses can attend, then they must attend. If a witness has difficulty getting time off work then a witness summons can be served. The courts will explain how to do this.

The final hearing

The final hearing is usually held in public but can be held in private if the parties agree or the judge thinks that it is necessary. Hearings in the small claims track are informal and the usual rules of evidence do not apply. The judge can adopt any method of dealing with the hearing that he or she thinks fit and can also ask questions of the witnesses before anyone else. A lay representative has the right to speak on behalf of a person at a hearing but only if that party attends the hearing. If an interpreter is needed, because English is not the first language then an experienced advisor should be consulted, or the court may be able to advise on this. At the end of the hearing the judge will pass judgement. The judge has to give reasons for the decision that he or she has arrived at. If the claimant wins, he or she will get the court fee back as well as the sum awarded. If the claimant loses no fees will be returned. However, it is unlikely that any other costs will have to be paid.

Appealing against a decision

A party may appeal against a judgement in the small claims track only if the court made a mistake in law or there was a serious irregularity in the proceedings. If a person wishes to appeal then a notice of appeal must be filed within 14 days. A fee is payable although this can be waived in cases of financial hardship. If you do wish to appeal a decision, it is very likely that you would need to consult a solicitor or an experienced advisor to help you.

Enforcement of orders

If a defendant does not pay, the claimant can go back to court and enforce that order. As we have seen, there are a number of remedies, such as bailiff, attachment of earnings and garnishee order. Another fee is involved when enforcing. The court will give you full details of different remedies and fees involved.

Ch. 5

Accidents and Compensation

This chapter deals with accidents to a person and the position following that accident. If you hurt or damage yourself or your property through your own negligence, there will be no one to claim from except yourself. However, if a person is injured as a result of the negligence of someone else, there may be a claim for damages against that person.

The general rule covering claiming damages against another is that you can claim damages if:

- You have been injured against someone else's failure to take precautions against causing possible injury to another or their possessions
- It was a situation where a reasonable person would have been aware of the risk of your being injured and
- He or she would have taken precautions to avoid the risk.

What to do after an accident has occurred

The main point is that if you think that you may be able to lodge a claim for compensation following an accident then you should act very quickly. Often, after an accident, a person may be too shaken or upset to act quickly. A person causing damage to another quite often knows that this is the case and will seize the advantage.

The following are the steps that should be followed:

- Make sure that you have the name and address of all witnesses to the accident and that the police are called
- Make sure that, if injuries are involved, these are examined by a doctor or hospital and that you have accurate records
- Make sure that you have detailed, photographic or sketched evidence relating to the actual scene of the accident
- Write out a full description and inform your insurers

When can a person sue?
To prove negligence, a person must show the following:

- It was reasonably foreseeable that harm would result from a failure to take care
- There was a duty of care owed to another and that duty was not discharged
- Damage or injury to persons or property from the failure to take reasonable care

Even if a person can establish all of the above, the person at fault may still be able to provide a defence, explained further on.

Time limits in which a person must claim for negligent acts
The law lays down time limits within which an individual must take legal proceedings in relation to negligence. For most civil claims the basic time limit is six years. However, in cases of personal injuries or death, there is a three year time limit, which runs from the date of the injury or when the individual knew of the injury. One of the important points here is that a person can claim from the date that they knew of the injury. So an injury, say from asbestosis, may have started to form many years ago, and over a period of years. However, the claim only has to be made within three years of knowing about the injury. Children can bring a claim for personal

injury in their own right within three years of their 18th birthday, Children under 18 years must sue through their parent or guardian on their behalf.

Civil and criminal proceedings

The main aim of criminal proceedings against another is to allocate blame and punish the wrongdoer. The aim of civil proceedings is to compensate a person for that wrongdoing. However, it is true that criminal courts can also order compensation in cases of negligence.

Alternative sources of compensation

Because the law imposes limitations on the time taken to claim and also because there is cost and expense involved in taking a case to court, many people wisely take out insurance. To take care of ourselves, we take out life policies, personal accident insurance, health policies, household and all risk policies and so on. To take care of other people we take out liability insurance. This means in case of accidents, there is a form of insurance that can compensate. Quite often, the only loss suffered by the person causing negligence is emotional. The consequences of what has happened stay with him or her for a long time, depending on the nature of the accident.

Defences to a claim of negligence

Even f it has been established that another person was legally at fault in causing you harm, he or she may have a successful defence to your claim. This can reduce or eliminate your chances of winning negligence cases. The most common defences are:

- Contributory negligence
- Voluntary assumption of risk
- Unavoidable accident

Only one of the above defences need apply.

Contributory negligence

It can be argued that the victim has contributed to the accident by acting in a way that exacerbated the problem. A classic case is where, if you have an accident with another vehicle and that vehicle was driving with no headlights, the fact that you are driving with dipped headlights means that you have contributed to the subsequent damage by not ensuring that other vehicles can be fully seen.

Voluntary assumption of risk

If you agree to run a risk, and an accident does occur then you may not be able to claim against another. This could happen, for example, where you accept a lift from someone who you know is drunk and there is subsequently a crash. You knew of the risk and therefore you will limit your claim for damages.

However, those who put up notices that try to absolve them against risk will find that they are invalid in law. Such notices may be in a car wash or shop and say something to the effect that accidents are not the liability of the owners. In this case, a risk is not being taken by you.

Unavoidable accidents

When an accident occurs because of something or some situation which could not have been foreseen and against which precautions could not have been taken, this undermines any claim for compensation. An example is where a traffic accident took place because of a sudden illness, which is not contributed to negligence.

The occupier's liability

Whether you can sue someone for an accident occurring in the home really depends on the nature of the accident. Accidents occur in the home for many reasons and it really depends on the cause and effect principle.

The fundamental rule when looking at accidents in the home is that the occupier, or person with legal responsibility for the premises, must exercise a reasonable degree of care to ensure that their premises are reasonably safe for others to use. The occupier may not only be a householder. The occupier is anyone with legal responsibility for any premises, be they swimming baths, libraries or residential property.

Only people who suffer physical injury or damage to property can claim. The occupier can be liable if the injury is caused indirectly by the dangerous state of the premises. The occupier's primary responsibility is to anyone who visits the premises as a guest, to do a job, or for some other lawful purpose, such as to carry out a repair. The liability for harm suffered on property also extends to people that you do not invite, such as authorised walkers. Ramblers, children tempted by some attraction, such as a pond or apple tree, trespassers and undesirables.

The extent of your duty and responsibility will diminish with each category.

Accidents in the street

The classic is where someone falls over on the highway or outside a railway station. You may hurt yourself or damage your belongings. If you do fall because of a loose or uneven paving slab, or fall into a pothole then the highways authority may be to blame.

Defining 'highway'

A highway comprises the road that you will cross (carriageway) and the footpath. Local highway authorities are:

- County councils
- Metropolitan borough councils outside London
- London Borough councils
- District councils or parish councils for unclassified roads, footpaths and bridleways

Motorways and trunk roads are responsibilities of the Department for Transport. All of these authorities maintain highways at public expense and are responsible to those who use them. If the accident was caused by a mains cover or ongoing maintenance and repair, the appropriate organisation to claim from may be the utility company, such as British Telecom.

When a local authority may be liable

The authority is only responsible for dangers arising from the condition of the highway. Not all accidents in streets are attributable to this. The liability of the highway authority is based on lack of due care. If the authority could not have known of the danger then it will have a defence.

The local authorities responsibility will also extend to lighting, objects in the street that could cause damage, and also failing to provide adequate warnings in any other situation that could lead to harm.

Accidents at work

Liability for the safety of the workforce is regulated by a fairly in depth framework of law. This includes Health and Safety law and also the law governing negligence. Obviously, in a workplace there is a greater risk to the individual, in particular depending on the nature and type of work undertaken.

If you are an employer, it is your legal responsibility to assess what potential harm your employers or others might face in the workplace. There is a requirement to decide on the necessary safety conditions and make sure that they are implemented. There are many heavy penalties facing employers who do not comply with legislation and general tests of reasonableness, from being closed down to being taking to an industrial tribunal.

Employers liability insurance

By law, employers must take out insurance to cover themselves against any claims for compensation from the employee. In addition, a public liability policy is taken out to cover the employer against any claims from other parties as a result of negligence. Insurers will inspect a business where there are known risks, such as a chemical factory and insist on compliance with standards, Failure to do so will nullify the policy.

Health and safety legislation

The Health and Safety at Work Act 1974 imposes a general duty on employers to ensure, so far as is reasonably possible, the health, safety and welfare at work of all employees. There are many regulations within the Act, which cover many specific types of business. So, in addition to the fundamental basic requirements that cover all workplaces, there are heavier regulations depending on the nature of the business.

Contributory negligence

Employees have a duty to co-operate with the employer to take care for their own and others safety. Employees who put their colleagues or members of the public at risk by carelessness or by disobeying safety instructions can also be deemed to be negligent and also liable for damages against another.

Staff at risk from the public

Employers can be held liable if they fail to take all reasonable steps to prevent and guard against the likelihood of risk to their employees. There are certain categories of people who are at risk more than others, such as benefits workers, nurses and so on. Any claim for compensation is usually in tandem with criminal action. Employees who are victims of criminal assault can also claim from the Criminal Injuries Compensation Board.

Medical accidents

In the same way as others who are bound by the general rules of negligence, doctors and dentists have to exercise a reasonable degree of skill so as not to cause foreseeable injury to their patients.

It is important to realise that medical accidents do occur without anyone to blame. A simple routine operation can go wrong because of the reaction of the patient. Compensation cannot be recovered in these cases because no one can say that any particular doctor or hospital is in the wrong.

In all cases, liability is based on lack of due care. In some cases, this is beyond argument. In others, not so clear cut.

Establishing cause and effect

It can be very difficult to establish cause and effect. Doctors are often loath to testify against fellow professionals in negligence suits, patients have to prove that the doctor failed to practice an acceptable standard of professional skill which is not easy for a lay person to establish or judge. In addition, courts tend to be more protective of doctors for fears of opening the floodgates to litigation. A victim of medical negligence, or accident has the additional problem of establishing that it was the doctors or hospitals negligence which resulted in the injury. This is a particular problem where the negligent conduct is said to be a *failure* to treat or to diagnose.

If you think that you may have a claim for medical negligence you will need to take legal advice to be able to further the claim. There are many legal practices who specialise in medical negligence and they will be able to tell you whether you can claim.

Defences to negligence

The doctors negligence may be based on failing to provide information to the patient or in failing to obtain the patients consent to treatment. In the case of a treatment that carries some risk, and information is given, then the doctors negligence is reduced in the case of accident. If no information was given, the patient will be able to sue.

If no consent at all has been given to a doctor to adopt a particular procedure the doctor is particularly liable.

Doctors have also been held to be liable for:

- Failing to investigate the patients medical history before administering further treatment
- Failing to provide adequate information so that those responsible for subsequent treatment are duly informed

Who is responsible?

NHS Treatment

For NHS treatment the health authority or self-governing hospital trust is responsible for any proven lapses in skill or care of its employees. It will not matter whose fault or error caused the accident.

In the case of a fee-paying patient, the doctor must be sued personally. If the injury was caused by negligent nursing care the private hospital is sued. All doctors carry insurance under special schemes.

General non-medical safety in hospitals

Security is a growing problem in hospitals. Numbers of people wander in and out of hospital premises for many reasons. However, there have been some horrific cases of injuries to patients in hospitals from outsiders. Again, the hospital is liable for a patient's safety.

Making a complaint

There is a complaints procedure for any person, patient or not, who wishes to lodge a complaint against a specific hospital or member of staff. This does not however, cover financial compensation. If financial compensation is being sought then legal action must be taken.

To use the complaints procedure a person must be a patient or former patient of the practitioner or institution concerned. It is possible to complain on behalf of existing or former patients but the hospital or practice must agree that the person complaining is a suitable representative.

A complaint must be made as soon as possible after the incident. The time limit for complaints is usually six months form the date of the incident. However, if a hospital or practice is unaware of there being any cause for complaint, the six month time limit begins from when they first became aware. This start date must be within twelve months of the date of the incident.

There is discretion to waive the limit where it would be unreasonable to expect the complaint to have been made in time, for example, because of grief or trauma. It must, however, still be possible to investigate the complaint. There are three stages in the complaints procedure:

- Local resolution
- Independent revue panel
- The Health Service Ombudsman

Local resolution

If a person wishes to make a complaint about any aspect of NHS treatment they have received or been refused, they should first go to the practice, hospital or trust concerned and ask for a copy of their complaints procedure.

Independent review panel

If local resolution fails to solve the matter then the matter should be referred to the trust or, in the case of a family practitioner, the local health authority or primary care trust for an independent review. The matter is then referred to a convenor who has a number of options in deciding how to proceed with a complaint:

They can:

- Refer the complaint back to the practice where the complaint began for further action under local resolution
- Arrange for both parties to attend conciliation
- Set up an independent review panel which will investigate the complaint
- Take no further action if it is felt that everything has been done that could be done
- If the person is still unhappy then the matter can be referred to the Health Service Ombudsman. There are three Ombudsman, one each for England, Wales and Scotland. The addresses of the Ombudsman can be obtained from any hospital or medical practice. The Ombudsman has far reaching powers at the highest levels and will investigate the complaint, set time limits and advise you accordingly. The decision of the Ombudsman is final.

****

Ch. 6

Consumer Protection Generally

Consumers are protected by both civil and criminal law. As we shall see below, the general law of contract gives some protection, especially from misrepresentation. There are special rules for consumer contracts, including:

- Contracts for buying goods
- Contracts for services
- Distance selling
- Other areas such as package holidays, insurance, food and finance

The tort of negligence gives limited protection where the consumer has no contractual rights. In addition, there is protection from defective goods under the Consumer Protection Act 1987. The criminal law also affords some protection against such matters as trade descriptions.

The law of contract

All transactions between consumers and suppliers are based on the law of contract. Every exchange of goods is an agreement between buyer and seller.

It therefore follows that underlying each exchange is an area of law which defines the rights and obligations of both buyer and seller. The purchaser and the person who sells goods and services are not free to do exactly as they wish after the sale or, indeed, make up the rules as they go along.

The major area of law which supported and assisted consumers was the Sale of Goods Act 1979, as amended by the Sale and Supply of Goods Act 1994. From October 1st 2015, the Consumer Rights Act has consolidated these Acts, along with the Unfair Terms in Consumer Contracts Regulations 1999.

The Consumer Rights Act 2015

Goods

Under the Consumer Rights Act 2015, all goods supplied under a consumer contract should:

- be of satisfactory quality;
- be fit for purpose;
- match the description, sample or model; and
- be installed correctly (if part of the contract).

Rights of a consumer to return goods Under the CRA 2015

There is an Initial rights to reject the goods – an automatic 30 day period to return the goods if they do not meet the implied terms unless the expected life of the goods is shorter than 30 days. This right entitles the consumer to a 100% refund.

Right to repair or replacement - If the 30-day period has lapsed or during that time, the consumer chooses not to exercise their right to reject goods, they will be entitled in the first instance to claim a repair or replacement. This remedy will be deemed a failure if, after one attempt at repair or replacement, the goods still do not meet the necessary requirements.

Right to a price reduction and final right to reject - If repair or replacement is unavailable or unsuccessful to the consumer, then they can claim a price reduction or a final right to reject the goods. The reduction or refund can be up to 100% of the product value.

Significant exclusions

Consumer rights are subject to the following exclusions:

- before contract, where defects are brought to the consumer's attention, or if the consumer examines the goods and any defects should have been obvious;
- where a consumer changes his/her mind about wanting the goods;
- if the product was used for a purpose that is neither obvious nor made known to the trader; or
- where faults have appeared as a result of fair wear and tear (only applicable 6 months after the goods are provided to the consumer).

Services

Like the implied terms that exist currently under Supply of Goods and Services Act, the services must be performed to a certain standard. Under the Consumer Rights Act, all services supplied under a consumer contract should:

- be carried out with reasonable care and skill;
- completed for a reasonable price (where no price is specified, i.e. hourly rates);
- completed within a reasonable time (where no timescale is provided); and
- completed in accordance with any information said or conveyed in writing to the consumer where the consumer relies on it (intended to include quotations, assurances regarding timescales and information provided pre-contract to the customer which induces them to purchase services from the trader). This is in addition to any rights that may arise as a result of a misrepresentation.

49

Rights of a consumer when services do not comply

Repeat performance of the services - when a provider fails to exercise reasonable care and skill or where requirement arising from information they gave about the service is breached. This Cannot be used where it would be impossible to finish providing service to the required standard.

Reduction of price - A price reduction can also be claimed where the service is not provided within a reasonable time; or the supplier breaches the terms given to consumers, whether orally or in writing regarding the standards of service. Can be up to 100% of agreed price.

Appointment of new supplier. Only in circumstances where getting the original supplier to do the work is impracticable or unreasonable, the consumer may have a claim for remedial work by another supplier.

Significant exclusions

Consumer rights are subject to the following exclusions:

- where unless agreed to the contrary, it does not achieve the consumer's desired outcome (provided trader uses reasonable care and skill);
- where it is the consumer who is responsible for things going wrong (supplier should always make notes of instructions);
- where damage is caused by the consumer.
- where the consumer simply changes their mind ; or
- where faults have appeared as a result of fair wear and tear.

Digital content

The Consumer Rights Act definition of digital content is: "data which [is] produced and supplied in digital form.

Any physical media that hosts digital content (such as a CD or Blu-ray) carrying faulty content is still subject to the Consumer Rights Act relating to goods, but content on that item will be governed by the digital content provisions of the Consumer Rights Act.

Under the Consumer Rights Act, digital content must be:

- of satisfactory quality (taking into account description of the content, the price paid and other circumstances such as labelling and advertising);
- fit for a particular purpose; and
- as described (including system requirements and another other information given to the original digital content). Upgrades can add to this description.

Most computer operating systems or games have minor bugs that are corrected over time with patches or upgrades and this will be tested objectively as what is "reasonable" to be deemed acceptable in the context of satisfactory quality.

Significant exclusions

Consumer rights are subject to the following exclusions:

- the consumer's attention was drawn to an unsatisfactory aspect of the digital content before a contract was made (for example if a game is in beta testing where bugs are typically accepted as part of the game);
- where the consumer examines the digital content before the contract is made and that examination ought to reveal the unsatisfactory aspect; or
- where a trial version is examined by the consumer before the contract is made and a reasonable examination of the trial product ought to make the unsatisfactory aspect apparent (for example, watermarks on files produced by the product).

Remedies under the Consumer Rights Act for defective digital content

Repair or replacement - the consumer does not have a choice of repair or replacement if it is either impossible to do so or disproportionate compared to another available remedy. If content is defective within six months of its supply, it is to be taken as being defective on the day it was supplied.

Price reduction - this is only triggered if the remedy of repair/replacement is not possible or where it has been requested and not provided within a reasonable time. The remedy may be up to the full cost of the digital content.

Other remedies

The following remedies can be claimed either in addition to, or instead of the remedies above:

- a claim for damages;
- forcing the supplier to perform the contract;
- a full refund; or
- not to pay for the product.

It should be noted that a consumer can never recover the same loss twice.

"Free" content

The Consumer Rights Act enables a consumer to be able to rely on the remedies provided for faulty or damaging 'free' digital content. For the consumer to be able to do this the digital content must be supplied under a contract where the consumer has to pay for goods, services or other digital content – computer magazines, for example, typically provide a 'free' CD with various software included with the magazine.

Damage to devices

Where digital content causes damage to a device or to other digital content (such as corrupting files), and that device or content belongs to the customer and the damage is a kind of which would not have occurred if the supplier had exercised reasonable skill, then one of the following remedies will be available to the consumer:

- repair of the damage, which must be done within a reasonable time, without significant inconvenience and without cost to the consumer; or
- payment of compensation, which must be given without undue delay, and in any event within 14 days of the trader agreeing to pay the compensation. The trader cannot charge the consumer a fee for this.

Unfair terms in contracts

The Consumer Rights Act replaces and adds to the current rules on unfair terms in consumer contracts under Unfair Contracts Terms Act 1977 ("UCTA") and Unfair Terms in Consumer Contracts Regulations 1999 ("UTCCR") in respect of consumer contracts. An unfair term of a consumer contract is not binding on the consumer, and the assessment of whether a term is unfair will continue to be based on whether the term under scrutiny causes a significant imbalance in the parties' rights and obligations under the contract, to the detriment of the consumer.

Whether a term is fair (or unfair) is to be determined by taking into account:

- the nature of the subject matter of the contract (i.e. the circumstances of the contract);
- reference to all the circumstances existing when the term was agreed; and

- to all of the other terms of the contract or of any other contract on which it depends.

The Consumer Rights Act will apply to consumer notices (whether contractual/non-contractual, oral or written) as well as consumer contracts in the typical form.

Restrictions on excluding liability

Although the Consumer Rights Act 2015 is not intended to prevent businesses from limiting liability in their entirety, businesses looking to include in their terms and conditions limitations should note the following:

- it is not possible to exclude or limit the application of the remedies for faulty goods and digital content (such as right to repair or replacement) that are implied into all consumer contracts under the Consumer Rights Act;
- the implied term that the services will be provided with reasonable skill and care cannot be excluded or limited for the reasons above; and
- whilst it is possible to limit liability for supply of services in respect of price and time for performance (provided that such a limit will not prevent the consumer from being able to recover the full contract price), any other limitations in respect of service performance would be subject to a test of fairness.

The act states that if goods turn out to not fulfill any of these criteria you have the right to demand a refund from the seller unless you have accepted the goods. The act provides that goods have been 'accepted' by the buyer where:

- you tell the seller you have accepted them
- you do something to or with them which prevents you from giving the goods back in their original state, such as alter, consume or damage them
- you keep the goods for 30 days without rejecting them

It is a good idea to report the problem to the seller as soon as you become aware of the fault. If you do wish to reject the goods you must give clear notice of this to the seller. If you allow 30 days to elapse then you no longer have the right to a refund, but you are still entitled to get the item repaired or replaced for free instead.

Faulty goods are also often covered by the manufacturer's guarantee or warranty, but this is in addition to your automatic rights retailer. Your rights may also extend beyond the manufacturer's guarantee once it has expired.

How to obtain refunds for faulty goods

If a fault develops soon after you purchased an item, or if it was faulty straight away, meaning the goods are not of satisfactory quality, then you are entitled to a full refund from the retailer.

The legal term to use here is the 'right to reject' under the Consumer Rights Act 2015 as the item was not of satisfactory quality. You must give the seller clear notice that the item is rejected within 30 days for a refund to be given.

To obtain a refund:

- Contact the retailer. Tell them you want to reject the item and would like a full refund. If the item is genuinely faulty and 30 days have not elapsed since the purchase, you should get a refund. You will probably need to provide proof of purchase but remember this doesn't always have to be a receipt. It can be a credit card or bank statement, a witness, a cheque stub or any other evidence that proves you bought the product from that retailer. If the retailer rejects your claim then check to see if the faulty goods are covered by the manufacturer's guarantee. If they are then tell the manufacturer about the fault and ask for a refund.

- If neither the retailer nor manufacturer offers a refund then write to the retailer again formally rejecting the faulty goods under the Consumer Rights Act 2015. Explain that you will take the matter to the small claims court unless a full refund is offered.

- If the retailer still does not offer a refund then after this then you may want to consider getting the item replaced or repaired instead. If, however, you are adamant that you want a refund, you may be able to take the case to the small claims court.

- If you paid for the faulty goods with a credit card and they cost between £100 and £30,000, the creditor card company will be jointly liable with the seller if the goods are not of satisfactory quality and you are entitled to a refund from either the seller or your credit card provider under Section 75 of the Consumer Credit Act. You can also use this method if the retailer goes out of business after you buy the faulty goods.

How to get faulty goods repaired or replaced

Under the Consumer Rights Act 2015, your consumer rights may allow you to get faulty goods repaired or replaced for free up to six years after purchase (five years in Scotland), although the longer you have had the goods the progressively more difficult it will be to show the defect arose as a result of the state of the goods at time of purchase.

If the fault arises within six months of the purchase, and it's not because of fair wear and tear, accidental damage or misuse, then the retailer must repair or replace the faulty goods. If the retailer objects, he must prove that the item wasn't faulty to begin with or that it wasn't expected to last very long.

If six months have passed and something goes wrong, you might still get a repair or replacement but you will have to prove that the goods were inherently faulty, i.e. show that there is no other cause, such as accidental damage, for the fault. To help you prove this, you may wish to obtain and independent expert's report to back up your claim, although these can be expensive. To get faulty goods repaired or replaced:

- Contact the retailer, tell them about the problem and ask for the goods to be either repaired or be replaced. You can specify which you'd prefer but it is ultimately a question of what is more economical from the perspective of the retailer.

You will probably need to provide proof of purchase but remember this doesn't always have to be a receipt. It can be a credit card or bank statement, a witness, a cheque stub or any other evidence that proves you bought the product from that retailer.

- Alternatively, if the faulty goods are still covered by their guarantee, contact the manufacturer, tell them about the problem and ask for the goods to be repaired or replaced.
- If the retailer or manufacturer do not help, write to the retailer and make a more formal request. Say that you are exercising your rights under the Consumer Rights Act 2015 as the item is not of "satisfactory quality" and you would like to have it repaired or replaced.

In your letter, warn the retailer that if it fails to accept to your demands you will start proceedings in the small claims track of the County Court.

- If your retailer still refuses to cooperate then consult our guide to taking a dispute to the County Court and consider taking that route. Bear in mind that you cannot take a case to court if you purchased the faulty goods more than six years ago.

Second-hand goods and sale items

The Consumer Rights Act 2015 also covers goods bought second hand, as we as goods bought at a discount price in a sale. However the requirement that goods be of satisfactory quality does not apply to a particular defect where:

- that particular defect has been pointed out to you before you agreed to buy the goods, and/or
- you inspect the goods before agreeing to buy them and the particular defect is one that you should really have spotted

The Consumer Protection Act 1987

An additional form of consumer protection is contained in the Consumer Protection Act 1987, which relates to the physical protection of the consumer and his/her property from the effects of faulty or defective products. A product is defective under the 1987 Act if it is not as safe as the average person would be entitled to expect.

Whether you buy or hire goods, they have to be safe. If you are injured by them in any way as a result of their hazardous nature, then the manufacturer and the importer (if it has come from outside the EU) are strictly liable for any damage or loss caused to you or those that used the product.

"Strict liability" means that you do not have to prove that they were at fault. What you will have to prove is that the product was defective, and that it was this defect that caused the injury, or in tragic cases, even death. Therefore, if you are injured when your car, whether it is your own, hired or being bought on HP, crashes due to a defect then you could sue the manufacturer for your injury and losses. However the Act only applies to damage caused to goods other than those that are defective, it does not allow you to claim for the cost of the defective goods themselves only the damage or injury caused to other goods or people by the defect.

Non receipt of goods and late delivery-Delivery rights

The retailer is responsible for goods until they are in your physical possession or in the possession of someone appointed by you to accept them. This means that retailers are liable for the service provided by the couriers they employ - the delivery firm is not liable. The retailer is responsible for the goods until they are delivered to you and in your possession.

Late deliveries

There is a default delivery period of 30 days during which the retailer needs to deliver unless a longer period has been agreed.

Guarantees and Warranties

In law, a guarantee is an agreement given by a trader to a consumer, without any extra charge, to repair, replace or refund on goods which do not meet the specifications set out in the guarantee. A warranty is an insurance policy which provides cover for the unexpected failure or breakdown of goods, usually after the manufacturer's or trader's guarantee has run out.

Guarantees and warranties are additional to the legal rights you have as a consumer and must not affect those rights in any way.

What is a guarantee?

In law, a guarantee is an agreement given by a trader to a consumer, without any extra charge, to repair, replace or refund goods that do not meet the specifications set out in the guarantee. A guarantee is usually issued by the manufacturer of goods or by a trader that provides goods as part of a service - replacement windows, for instance. Generally, a guarantee provider undertakes to carry out free repairs, for a set period of time, for problems that can be attributed to manufacturing defects.

An insurance backed guarantee provides the consumer with protection if the trader that provided the goods or service under guarantee ceases to trade and can no longer fulfil its obligations under the guarantee. The insurance company underwrites the terms of the guarantee for the remainder of the guarantee period.

A guarantee is additional to the legal rights you have as a consumer and must not affect those rights in any way.

What is a warranty?

A warranty (or extended warranty) is broadly defined in law as a contract for cover for goods, which is entered into by a consumer for (money) monetary consideration. A warranty is a form of insurance policy which provides cover for the unexpected failure or breakdown of goods, usually after the manufacturer's or trader's guarantee has run out. Some warranties are service contracts rather than insurance backed (you should check the status of the warranty before you purchase it) . Warranties can vary - they offer different protection, from the most basic cover to those which provide comprehensive cover. For instance, you may be covered only for the 'market value' of the goods, which means their second hand value after use or you may be covered 'new for old'. Do not assume that a warranty will provide cover for all problems encountered with the goods. They usually have exclusions that set limits on the cover you receive.

A warranty or extended warranty is additional to the legal rights you have as a consumer and must not affect those rights in any way.

What legal protection do I get with warranties and guarantees?

The Sale and Supply of Goods to Consumers Regulations 2002 states that if a guarantee provider offers a guarantee on goods sold or supplied to consumers, the provider takes on a contractual obligation to honour the conditions set out in the guarantee. For example, if the guarantee provider refuses to repair goods as set out under the terms of the guarantee, you can take legal action against the provider of the guarantee for breach of contract. This could be claiming back the cost of repairs if you have had them carried out elsewhere.

The guarantee should be written in English and the terms should be set out in plain intelligible language. The name and address of the guarantee provider, the duration of the guarantee and the location it covers must also be given. You have the right to ask the provider to make the guarantee available to you in writing or any other durable form available.

If you have a problem with an insurance backed extended warranty that was sold to you, and you have been unable to resolve it with the warranty provider, you are entitled to take your complaint to the Financial Ombudsman Service. For problems with non insurance backed extended warranties, contact the Citizens Advice consumer service.

The Supply of Extended Warranties on Domestic Electrical Goods Order 2005 requires traders that supply extended warranties on domestic electrical goods to provide consumers with certain information before the sale of the extended warranty.

Traders supplying this type of extended warranty are required to:

- clearly display the price and duration of the warranty
- make it clear that the warranty is optional
- give you information on your statutory rights
- inform you that the warranty does not have to be purchased at the time the goods are purchased
- provide details of cancellation and termination rights
- inform you that warranties may be available elsewhere
- provide a statement on the financial protection consumers have if the provider of the extended warranty goes out of business

- state whether or not the warranty will cease if a claim is made
- inform you that your household insurance may be relevant to the purchase of the goods
- give a quotation in writing and inform you that the quotation price is valid for at least 30 days if the warranty costs more than £20
- allow you to cancel it within 45 days and get a refund if a claim has not been made and if the warranty that was supplied has an initial duration of more than one year
- allow you to cancel it and receive a pro rata refund after 45 days even if a claim has been made and if the warranty that was supplied has an initial duration of more than one year

If insurance backed guarantees and warranties are marketed and sold at a distance - without face to face contact between the consumer and trader, such as online - the Financial Services (Distance Marketing) Regulations 2004 apply. These regulations cover the distance marketing of consumer financial services and specify the information that must be given to you before and after a contract is concluded. You have the right to cancel a financial services distance contract and the cancellation period for this type of insurance is 14 calendar days which runs from the day after the day the contract is concluded. Guarantees and warranties are in addition to the statutory rights you have under the Consumer Rights Act 2015.

Package Holidays

There are various common law protections in the case of holidays. However, the main area of consumer protection in the case of package holidays are the Package Travel, Package Holidays and Package Tours Regulations 1992 and the ABTA Code of practice.

The Regulations were introduced to comply with EU Directive 90/314 on Package Holidays and Package Tours. The directive was inevitable because of the level of tourism across EU member states. Most consumer problems related to holidays concern differences between the holiday description on booking and the actual reality. It is possible in these circumstances that there is also an offence under s14 Trade Descriptions Act 1978.

The Package Travel, Package Holidays and Package Tours Regulations 1992-The definition of 'package holidays'.

The Regulations do not alter the existing common-law protections but add significant duties on tour operators. The Regulations apply to all package holidays-but the word 'package' is given a very broad definition in Regulation 2 (1): the prearranged combination of at least two of the following components when sold or offered for sale at an inclusive price and when the service covers a period of more than 24 hours or includes overnight accommodation:

a) transport
b) accommodation
c) other tourist services not ancillary to transport or accommodation and accounting for a significant proportion of the package and
i) submission of separate accounts for different components shall not cause the arrangement to be other than a package
ii) the fact that a combination is arranged at the request of the consumer in accordance with his specific instructions (whether modified or not) shall not of itself cause it to be treated as other than prearranged,

Information to be given by the holiday operator before the contract is concluded

The basic common law rules on formation can apply. The brochure is generally seen as an invitation to treat. But the Regulations, in Regulation

9, provide certain safeguards by ensuring that certain information is given to the consumer before the contract is concluded, and that the information is comprehensible to the consumer. The necessary information is detailed in schedule 2:

- the intended destination
- the intended means of travel
- the exact dates and the place of departure
- the locality of accommodation and its classification
- meals that are included in the package
- the minimum number of travellers to allow the holiday to go ahead
- any relevant itineraries, visits or excursions
- the names and full addresses of the organiser, retailer and insurer
- the price and any details with regard to revising the price
- the payment schedule and method of payment
- any other necessary details, such as specific arrangements for diet etc, that have been indicated by the consumer
- the method and period for complaints to be made.

This information must be given to the consumer both before the contract is made and in the contract itself. This will not apply to late bookings. Failure to comply is a breach under regulation 9(3) and the operator is then prevented from relying on terms that are not sufficiently explained in this way - and the consumer may also cancel the holiday.

Statements made in holiday brochures

The common law distinction between terms and 'trade puffs' applies where no reasonable person could rely on the statement. But, in any case, by regulation 4, holiday operators will be liable if they supply misleading information in their descriptive matter.

Liability-Terms and performance of the contract

By regulation 15(1) the operator is liable for the improper performance of the contract by other service providers. The only exception is where the improper performance is neither the fault of the operator nor of any other service provider:

- including where it is the fault of the consumer
- or where it is caused by the unforeseeable and unavoidable act of the third party; and
- where forces majeure applies, e.g. hurricanes

The ABTA Code of Practice also requires that it should be a term of all contracts for package holidays that the operator will accept liability for the acts or omissions of their employees, agents, sub-contractors and suppliers which results in death, injury or illness-and that the operators will offer advice, guidance and financial assistance of up to £5000 to consumers on holiday who suffer death, injury or illness.

Alterations to the holiday

Alteration depends on the terms of the contract-a common term allows alteration to the itinerary. If an alteration amounts to non-performance then it is a breach of the contract by the operator and will be classed as a breach of the condition allowing the consumer to repudiate and claim back the cost of the holiday.

The ABTA Code Clause 2.4 requires operators to offer suitable alternatives in the case of cancellation or alteration.

Overbooking of flights

Passengers who are denied travel because of overbooking are entitled to a choice/combination of:

65

- reimbursement of the cost of the ticket
- re-routing to the destination at the earliest moment
- re-routing at a later date, at the passengers convenience
- compensation

There are special rules applying to overbooked flights from airports in the European Union. The rules also apply to flights from airports outside the EU but flying into an EU airport, on an EU airline.

These rules apply only if you were not allowed to board the flight, not if you volunteered to take a different flight. You must have a valid ticket and have met check in deadlines at the airport. If these conditions are met then you will be entitled to a full refund of your ticket and a free return flight to your first point of departure, if needed, or another flight either as soon as possible or at a later date of your choice. You will also be entitled to:

- compensation. The amount you get will depend on the circumstances, i.e. how late you were as a result of the overbooking
- compensation for two telephone calls, e mails or other forms of communication
- reasonable meals and refreshments if you have to wait for a later flight
- Hotel accommodation if appropriate (stay overnight until next flight)

If the above EU rules don't apply then you should check the terms and conditions with the operator.

Remember, the law applies to this area as it does to all other areas and the operator cannot opt out. If you are not satisfied with what has happened then you should contact ABTA who run an arbitration scheme (address at the back of the book).

You can also contact the Association of Independent Tour Operators on www.abta.com.

Insolvency of the tour operator

The Package Travel, Package Holidays and package Tours Regulations 1992 apply. Under regulation 16(1) tour operators must at all times be able to satisfy evidence of sufficient funds to be able to return deposits in the event of insolvency. Consumers who pay by credit card are also protected under the Consumer Credit Act 1974.

ABTA bonding arrangements ensure that a consumer is not left stranded when a tour operator goes into insolvency during his/her holidays.

Remedies

Damages are usually awarded on the basis of difference in value between what was contracted for and what was provided. Incidental losses are also possible. Claims are also possible for physical discomfort. Operators are, basically, liable for all losses that arise from the breach.

Consumers and Credit

The most important Act dealing with consumers and credit is the Consumer Credit Act 1974. This act also encompasses loans from pawnbrokers and also payday loans. This has been supplemented by the Consumer Credit (Advertising) Regulations 2011 (see further on in this chapter).

Nowadays, many people use credit to help them with their buying. It helps to spread the load, especially with expensive items such as furniture or cars. But borrowing can be costly and with so many different types of credit available, it is wise to shop around before you sign any credit agreement.

Using a credit card when buying a single item costing over £100 but under £30,000 can provide extra protection if you have a problem with your purchase. Whether you use your credit card to pay the full amount or even part of the deposit (as little as £1 but no more than £25,000), the credit card company is legally bound to help in cases of faulty goods or non-delivery if the retailer goes out of business.

Try to avoid interest charges by paying your credit card bill off in full when it arrives. Be warned, however, that you may not be protected if your payment is made through a third party - see the section below on credit cards.

What the law says

The main law to give you protection when buying on credit is the Consumer Credit Act 1974. By law you're entitled to a copy of your credit agreement so make sure you get one. Never sign a blank form or even leave some sections blank.

Right of withdrawal

You have a right to withdraw from a credit agreement without giving any reason, within 14 days. When the 14 day period begins will depend on when the agreement is made and there must be information in the agreement telling you about your withdrawal rights. On withdrawal you must repay the amount of money received and any interest accrued.

Credit cards

Under section 75 of the Consumer Credit Act 1974, if you use your credit card to buy a single item costing more than £100 but no more than £30,000, you can claim from the credit card company or the trader if something goes wrong. Many websites use an online payment processor such as Paypal, Worldpay or Google Checkout. While the law in this area is not certain, you may not be covered by the protection offered by section 75. Online payment processors do have their own refund systems, so make sure you read their terms and conditions carefully. If you use a credit card to buy airline or other travel tickets from a travel agent you cannot normally claim against the travel agent if the airline delays or cancels the flight as they were contracted to supply the ticket, not the flight. However, if you use a credit card to buy the travel agent's own package of travel arrangements the agent then becomes the supplier of the holiday package and has equal liability with the credit card company.

Credit reference agencies

You don't have a right to credit. Before giving you credit, lenders want to check whether you're an acceptable risk. To help them do this they may check with firms called Credit Reference Agencies (CRAs). These agencies don't keep 'black lists' or give an opinion as to whether or not you should be given credit. They just provide information about your credit record. You are entitled to see a copy of any information they hold on you and to correct anything in it that you can prove is wrong. You are entitled to see a copy of your file if you make a written request and send £2. Online and telephone requests may cost more. The contact details of the credit reference agencies are shown below and you can also find more information on the website of the Money Advice Service. The CRA commits a criminal offence if it fails to correct files.

Credit unions

To borrow from a credit union you must first become a member and show by saving regularly over a set period that you will be able to afford the repayments. This is an excellent way of getting credit as the interest rate is usually lower than that used by other lenders.

Hire purchase

You cannot end a hire purchase agreement unless you are up to date with your payments. You will have to pay at least half of the total hire purchase price. You cannot sell the goods until the agreement has been paid off.

Logbook loans

Consumers will regularly see these loans being advertised on the high street or on the internet promising cash fast, but they can often prove to be more problematic than beneficial for borrowers. A logbook loan is a loan secured on your vehicle. You will be asked to hand over the logbook (V5 form - vehicle registration document) and sign a document called a bill of sale. This means that the protection provided by the Consumer Credit Act – that cars cannot be seized without a court order – is removed and the lender can then seize the car if the loan is not paid.

The bill of sale also transfers temporary ownership of your vehicle to the lender, but you are still able to use it while you are making the loan repayments. You only become the legal owner of the vehicle once again when you have settled the agreement in full.

Consumers should consider other types of borrowing before agreeing to a logbook loan, especially if you cannot do without your vehicle. Although these loans provide quick access to money, the APR is likely to be very high, commonly over 200% APR. There may be cheaper ways you can borrow, which do not put you at such a risk of losing your assets. The concept of a logbook loan can be complicated, so if you plan to take one out make sure you ask the lender to explain anything you do not understand. It is vitally important you understand your responsibilities under the agreement to help you minimise the risk of losing your vehicle.

Furthermore, the law only recognises the bill of sale if the lender registers it with the High Court. If it is not registered, the lender must get a court's approval to repossess your vehicle. So if you think you may fall behind with your loan repayments and want to know what will happen to your vehicle, you will need to check if the bill of sale is registered. You will need to give both your and your lender's name and address along with a small fee to the High Court.

Money lenders

They charge high interest rates and you should be very careful with this type of credit. Avoid anyone who simply calls at your home or speaks to you in the pub and offers you a loan: they are committing a criminal offence. Money leaders may ask for some security for the loan. If they do, never give them your child benefit book or other social security book.

Payday loans

Consumers unable to access credit through traditional banking means are increasingly turning to alternative sources, including payday loan companies. Payday, or paycheque loans, are short-term loans that you get in return for your pay cheque or proof of your income. They are basically cash advances on the salary you are expecting and are available online and on the high street.

They can be a way of getting your hands on your wages quicker than you otherwise would, but it is important to be aware of the high interest rates charged and the consequences of falling behind with your repayment.

This type of borrowing is not suitable for those looking to repay their loans over a long period, as they are designed to be short-term loans to deal with short-term personal cash flow issues. If loans are rolled over, debts could escalate and consumers could get into difficulties. They should only be considered if consumers are confident that they'll be able to repay the debt in full when it is due.

If you are considering using a payday loan company, you should look into all the available alternatives first:

- Speak to your bank manager as you may be able to get an agreed overdraft
- Look into Social Fund Loans - these are government-funded, interest-free loans available to those on low incomes
- Check out your local credit union.

If you have no alternative to a payday loan make sure:

- You fully understand the costs and charges involved as rates higher than 1,000% APR are common
- You do not borrow more than you can repay or for longer than necessary. If you miss the repayment, the cost of borrowing even a small amount can become very high, very quickly

If consumers find themselves relying on payday loans regularly they may find it useful to re-examine their household budget.

Changes to payday loan regulation

On 1st April, 2014, the FCA (Financial Conduct Authority) took over regulation of the consumer credit market from the OFT (Office of Fair Trading). One of the first things the FCA did was to crack down on lenders that offer 'High Cost Short Term Credit' (HCSTC), and this includes payday loans. The key changes include:

Limiting the number of times a loan can be rolled over

Currently if you can't afford to repay your payday loan on time you can usually roll it over to the next month. This flexibility comes as a cost and can quickly lead to a small short term loan turning into a hefty loan term debt.

Usually the balance of your loan is extended by a month, with extra interest and roll over fees whacked on to your borrowing. You generally only have to pay the interest charges upfront when you roll over a loan - but sometimes this can be rolled over as well.

Stopping lenders from trying to collect payment more than twice

Most payday lenders will use a CPA (Continuous Payment Authority) to collect payment. This is a way of taking money from your bank account

72

that gives the lender the right to take payment on any date they like, and any amount they like. This is important because although lenders should let you know when they plan to take payment and how much it'll be, not all do.

CPAs can be a quick and flexible way to pay your bills as they help you avoid default and late payment charges if the lender tries to collect payment from your account and the money isn't there. However, there is growing concern that they are open to misuse, leading to payday lenders taking money from their customers' accounts without warning.

This causes problems if money is taken ahead of other bills, causing defaults on more important debts like your council tax, utilities, mortgage or rent; and leading to bank charges and future credit issues. Under the new FCA rules, lenders will be limited to only two failed CPA attempts. This means that they can't continually try to withdraw money from your account when you don't have the funds available, and instead will need to contact you to find out what's going on. This limit can be reset if you decide to refinance or roll over your loan and pay the amount you currently owe.

Banning part payments by CPA

As well as introducing a limit on the number of times lenders can try to collect payment via CPA, they'll also be limited to how much they're able to collect.

In addition, caps will be introduced from 2nd January 2015 which will limit the amount of interest that can be charged. They are as follows:

- Initial cap of 0.8% a day in interest charges. Someone who takes out a loan of £100 over 30 days, and pays back on time, will therefore pay no more than £24 in interest

- A cap of £15 on the one-off default fee. Borrowers who fail to pay back on time can be charged a maximum of £15, plus a maximum of 0.8% a day in interest and fees
- Total cost cap of 100%. If a borrower defaults, the interest on the debt will build up, but he or she will never have to pay back more than twice the amount they borrowed

Personal loans

Shop around for the best value. Always consider how long it will take you to pay back the loan and how much you will pay in total, as well as how much your monthly payments are. Always check the Annual Percentage Rate (APR) being charged. It is the best way of comparing one deal with another. Generally, the lower the APR, the better the deal.

What to do if you have a complaint

Even if you think the goods are faulty, don't stop your payments or you could end up in trouble. See the shop manager at once and let your finance company know about the problem. If you can't sort it out yourself you should ask for advice from Consumerline on 0300 123 6262, your local Advice Centre or Citizens Advice.

****

Ch.7

Children And Adults

Parents Rights and obligations

Definition of a parent

The actual legal definition of a parent has been the subject of debate over the years. Whether the parent is a biological parent or psychological parent.

Biological parents

The law has traditionally approached the question of parentage by considering the biological link between adult and child as preferable. The law will rarely interfere with the authority of the biological parent, unless some other arrangement is preferable. In Re KD (a minor) (Ward: termination of access) 1988, Lord Templeman stated:

'The best person to bring up a child is the natural parent. It matters not whether the parent is wise or foolish, rich or poor, educated or illiterate, providing the child's moral and physical health is not endangered'.

There are two exceptions to this presumption: where the child is adopted (Adoption Act 1976 s39) and secondly where reproduction and childbirth follows on from sperm or egg donation (Human Fertilisation and Embryology Act 2008). Adoption will terminate the legal (parental) responsibility of natural parents towards the child and also extinguishes any rights a parent may have over a child. Where a person donates genetic material (eggs, sperm, embryos) he relinquishes any rights o biological parentage in relation to any child that may be born as a result.

Psychological parents
Good parenting depends very much on the ability to form an emotional/psychological bond with a child. A strong attachment between parent and child is considered to be an indicator of a stable and emotionally healthy relationship.

This bond is not exclusive to the biological parent but can form with a number of people, such as foster and adoptive parents. The courts have recognised the possibility of the independence of the biological and psychological relationship.

The legal parent
A parent, in the eyes of the law is a person who has responsibility for a child. Parental responsibility means 'all the rights, duties, powers, responsibilities and authorities which by law a parent has in relation to the child and his property' (Children Act 1989 s3). Legal parenthood carries the right and responsibility to register a child's name within six months of its birth and apply for residence/contact orders, specific issue orders, change the child's name and to apply for a prohibited steps order to prevent the removal of the child from the country.

A parent is the natural mother or natural father of the child. However, not all fathers have parental responsibility for their child and other parties may also have parental responsibility for the child. In addition, the local authority may have parental responsibility for the child where the child is in care, and foster parents may have responsibility. More than one person can have parental responsibility for a child (CA 1989 s 2(5)). Where other parties have parental responsibility for the child, this will only last for the duration of the order made in their favour.

Parental responsibility

Any person who is a legal parent has parental responsibility. In accordance with the Children Act 1989, s2, more than one person may have responsibility for the child at any one time. Thus, parental responsibility is shared in the case of a married couple and is shared where parents are separated. In cases where children are taken into care, the natural parents will still have parental responsibility: the responsibility will simply be shared with foster parents.

The following outlines who has parental responsibility:

- The mother has automatic parental responsibility (whether a child is born within or out of marriage s 33 Human Fertilisation and Embryology Act 2008);
- The married father;
- The unmarried father has automatic responsibility if the Adoption and Children Act 2002 s111(2)(a)(c) applies;
- The unmarried father if he is granted a court order under the Children Act 1989, s4;
- The adoptive parents of an adoptive child;
- If a child is a ward of court the court stands in the position of parents and a court in wardship has parented responsibility;
- A guardian appointed by a parent by deed or will has parental responsibility after the parents death;
- The Children's Act 1989 created the institution of custodianship, under which many parental rights are given to the foster parent but some rights remain with the natural parent.

Proving parentage

In cases where the identity of the biological father is unknown and the mother wishes to establish parentage, or the child or father wishes to dispute parentage, an order for a declaration of paternity (under the Family

Law Act) 1986, s55A, as amended by the Child Support, Pensions and Social Security Act 2000, s83(2) may be made. However, blood testing will only be ordered if it is considered to be in the child's best interests. In re O; Re J (children) (Blood Tests: Constraint) (2000) in two separate cases, a male applicant had obtained an order under s 20 (1) of the Family Law Reform Act 1969 for the use of blood tests designed to determine the paternity of a child who was the subject of the proceedings. In each case, the mother, whose consent was required under s 21(3) of the 1969 Act, refused to consent to the child's blood being tested. The court held that it was a matter for the mother to grant or withhold consent.

The courts, however, can order a blood test to be taken if it considers this to be in the best interests of child.

Step-parents

Where a parent remarries, the new spouse becomes the step-parent of any children of the previously married partner. Under the Adoption and Children's Act 2002, amending the Children's Act 1989 s 4(A)1:

Where a child's parent (A) who has parental responsibility for the child is married to a person who is not the child's parent (step parent) (a) parent A or, if the other parent of the child also has parental responsibility for the child, both parents may, by agreement with the step-parent provide for the step-parent to have parental responsibility for the child or (b) the court may, on application of the step-parent, order that the step-parent shall have parental responsibility for the child.

The Civil Partnership Act 2004 provides that civil partners will be eligible to apply for parental responsibility on the same basis as step parents.

Adoptive parents

An order of the court placing a child for adoption establishes the adoptive parent as the legal parent. The ACA 2002, s 46(1) states:

78

1) an adoption order is an order made by the court on an application under s 50 or 51 giving parental responsibility for a child to the adopters or adopter.

2) The making of an adoption order operates to extinguish the parental responsibility which any person other than the adopters or adopter has for the adopted child immediately before the making of the order.

Foster parents

When a child is in care of the local authority, he or she will be placed with foster carers. This can be a single adult or an adult couple in a family arrangement.

Parents and reproductive technology

The Human Fertilisation and Embryology Act 2008 came into effect on 13th November 2008 and amends the HFEA 1990. The key provisions of the 2008 Act are to:

- Ensure that all human embryos outside the body-whatever the process used in their creation-are subject to regulation.

- Ensure regulation of "human-admixed" embryos created from a combination of human and animal genetic material for research.

- Ban sex-selection of offspring for non-medical reasons. Sex selection is allowed for medical reasons.

- Recognise same sex couples as legal parents of children conceived through the use of donated sperm, eggs or embryos.

- Retain a duty to take account of the welfare of the child in providing fertility treatment, but replace the reference to "the need for a father" with the "need for supportive parenting"-hence valuing the role of all parents.

- Alter the restrictions on the use of HFEA-collected data to help enable follow up research of infertility treatment.

Under the Human Fertilisation and Embryology Act (HFEA) 2008, where a person has donated sperm or eggs then he or she relinquishes any rights over the genetic material. The HFEA determines the legal parent as a result of a child born from IVF treatment. The HFEA 2008, defines a 'mother' as 'the woman who is carrying or who has carried a child as a result of the placing in her of an embryo, or of sperm or eggs'.

Section 28 defines a father as being married to the woman 'at the time of placing in her of an embryo or the sperm or the eggs or of her insemination' unless it is shown that he did not consent to the placing in her of the embryo, sperm or eggs or to her insemination.

The Human Fertilisation and Embryology Authority (Disclosure of Donor) Regulations 2004

These regulations were passed to acknowledge a child's rights to know their genetic parentage. This is an important part of a child's identity. However, correspondingly, there is no obligation on the parents to tell the child that they were conceived using donated sperm.

Parties separating

When parties who consented to the placement of genetic material in the woman separate, a specific legal position arises. In the case of Re R (a child) (IVF Paternity of Child) 2005, the mother, A, and her partner B, were unmarried and sought IVF treatment which involved the fertilisation of A's eggs with sperm from a donor. In accordance with IVF procedure, B signed a form acknowledging that he would be the father of any child born in consequence. However, A nd B had already separated when implementation in A had taken place, about which B had no knowledge.

On an application by B, the judge declared under HFEA 1990, s28(3) that B was the legal father of the resulting child.

The court of appeal allowed A's appeal. B appealed and the House of Lords dismissed the ruling of the court of appeal holding:

'that section 28(3) of the HFEA should only apply to cases falling clearly within it and the legal relationship of a parent should not be based on a fiction, especially where deception was involved: that the embryo had to have been placed in the woman when treatment services were provided for her and the man together; and that, although they had originally been so provided for A and B, they had not been when implementation took place'.

Parental responsibility and childrens rights generally-Rights of Children in Domestic and International Law
The dominant statute governing the position of children in the UK is the Children Act 1989. This act sets out the fundamental premise of decisions taken in relation to children, which is the welfare principle. This provides that where decisions involving children are to be taken, the best interests of the children are the paramount consideration. The welfare principle has historically guided the development of children's law in the UK, and is the most significant restriction on children's autonomy and ability to exercise their rights independently. It is addressed in more detail below.

Further to the government's 'Every Child Matters' agenda, The Children's Act (CA) 2004 received royal assent in November 2004. The 2004 act codified 'five outcomes' for children, being their rights to:

- Be healthy
- Stay safe
- Enjoy and achieve

- Make a positive contribution
- Achieve economic well-being

The CA 2004 created a Children's Commissioner, and imposed enforceable duties on local authorities and other relevant bodies such as the police, NHS health services etc to work together in the provision of children's services.

Every Children's Services Authority (local authority) is required to publish a Children and Young People's Plan. This plan should show how the authority intends to enable children in their area to meet the five outcomes, and must be regularly reviewed. The European Convention on Human Rights (ECHR) has been incorporated into UK law, and is relevant to the rights of children and young people in much the same way as it is to those of adults. In addition, where the ECHR rights of a competent child are infringed simply by reason of their being a child, the anti-discrimination provisions in Article 14 may be applicable.

Key Areas of Parental Responsibility
Consultation with Children
Parents (and others exercising parental responsibility) are not legally obliged to consult their children as to their wishes or to involve them in decision making processes.

However, the exercise of parental responsibility is limited when children have sufficient understanding and capacity to make decisions about their own future. This was confirmed in the 1985 decision in *Gillick v Wisbeach Health Authority*, in which the House of Lords decided that a child under 16 could consent to medical treatment if he or she could understand what was involved in such treatment and was capable of expressing his or her views and wishes. This has come to be known as 'Gillick competence' and while the House of Lords did not identify a specific age at which children were to be deemed to be sufficiently mature to have their views considered, it follows from Gillick that the older the child, the greater the weight that will be attached to their views. This approach is consistent with certain provisions of the UNCRC – Article 5 which requires that children's rights be exercised in accordance with their evolving capacities and Article 12 which requires that in all decisions effecting children due weight should be attached to their views.

In 2006 the High Court applying Gillick, confirmed that young people were entitled to confidential advice or treatment on sexual matters, which includes abortion, without the knowledge or consent of their parents. This position does not breach the child's parent's rights to private and family life under Article 8 ECHR.

Names

A child's parents have an unfettered right to name their child and are required by law to register the child's name within 42 days of the child's birth. Where only one person has parental responsibility that person can change the child's name (e.g by deed poll) without requiring the consent or permission of anyone else. Where there is more than one person with parental responsibility and dispute as to change of name then it will be necessary to seek the court's permission. The court will consider a range of factors but the paramount consideration will be the welfare of the child. The opinions of a older child are likely to be highly relevant. A change of name is considered to be serious step, relating as it does to a child's identity.

Where a child becomes the subject of an adoption order, the adoptive parents acquire parental responsibility and have an absolute right to change a child's name.

With parental consent a child may use a different name from that on their birth certificate. A child of sixteen may change their name without their parent's consent. (A parent may apply to court in an attempt to prevent this but is unlikely to be successful). Equally, a child with sufficient maturity and understanding who is under the age of sixteen may apply to the court for permission.

Religion

A child who is sufficiently mature in accordance with the Gillick principles is entitled to choose his or her own religion. Where a dispute arises either between parents or between parents and the child over the choice of religious upbringing, the paramountcy of the child's welfare will prevail in resolving the conflict. If a parent seeks to impose a particular religion on a child it will not be tolerated if it causes harm to the child. Article 9 of the ECHR protects the right to freedom of thought, conscience and religion. (See also education, below).

Medical Treatment

In most cases it will be the parents who consent to medical treatment on behalf of their child. A child/young person can give valid consent provided the person providing treatment is of the view that he or she understands the nature and consequences of the treatment (ie that they are Gillick competent). At the time of writing the General Medical Council were seeking the views of children and young people in order to draft guidance to doctors as to the treatment of children.

Children under 18 may also refuse medical treatment but under the wardship jurisdiction a court can order medical treatment, including termination of a pregnancy or sterilisation, if it is deemed necessary in the child's best interests. This power is most commonly used in cases where a young person refuses life saving medical treatment due as a consequence of an eating disorder or mental illness.

The ECHR has decided that compulsory medical treatment for the purposes of preventing death or serious injury does not amount to inhuman or degrading treatment contrary to Article 3 ECHR where a patient is not capable of giving consent.

Consent to Marriage

There is no specific criminal offence of forced marriage, although the Foreign and Commonwealth Office deal with cases of UK children as young as 13 being forced into marriage.

A marriage where one party is under 16 is void. Young people between 16 and 18 may marry with parental consent. If the parents are separated or divorced the consent of both parents is necessary and if the child is in the care of the local authority it is necessary to obtain the consent of all persons having parental responsibility for the child.

Article 12 of the Convention protects the right of men and women of 'marriageable age' to marry. The prohibition on the marriage of children under 16 years does not infringe the right to marry because Article 12 clearly permits states to regulate the age at which a person is able to marry. Similarly, it is not possible to enter into a civil partnership if under the age of 16. A young person of 16 or 17 may only register a civil partnership with the consent of their parents.

Corporal Punishment

In international law physical punishment of children is totally prohibited. However, in the UK parents still have the right to administer reasonable physical chastisement to a child. It is possible to defend a charge of common assault against a child on the basis that the force used was no more than reasonable punishment. This position has been strongly criticised by the UN Committee, and by the Children's Commissioners for England, Wales, Scotland and Northern Ireland, who in 2006 issued a joint statement condemning the UK's position and calling for an outright ban on the physical punishment of children.

Corporal punishment is prohibited as a form of punishment in all other circumstances including as a punishment following conviction for an offence, in education and in care or foster homes.

In 2005 the UK House of Lords held that the ban on corporal punishment in independent schools did not amount to a breach of the parents' rights under Articles 8 and 9 ECHR. Parliament was bound to respect a religious belief in corporal punishment in school, but entitled to legislate in children's best interests against the manifestation of that belief.

Leaving Home

Generally, young people under 16 cannot leave home unless their parents agree.. The law relating to 16 to 17 year olds is not clear but it appears that they probably can leave home without parental consent. In theory, parents can apply to court for the return home of a child under 18 by seeking an injunction in wardship proceedings or a residence order. However, a court is extremely unlikely to order a child of 16 to 17 to return home against his or her wishes.

A court may make a residence order in favour of another adult if this is deemed to be in the child's best interests. This can be done on the adult's application or by the child if he or she is deemed to have sufficient understanding. The leave of the court is required,

Police will return a runaway child under 16 to his or her parents or to the local authority if he or she is in care unless they have reasonable cause to believe the child is in danger or at risk. In such circumstances the police may hold the child in police protection. The police then liaise with social services as to whether further action should be taken to protect the child. The police are unlikely to return a child over the age of 16 to his or her parents.

Ages of Consent

The legal definition of childhood remains quite fluid, and while children do not acquire full independence until they reach the age of 18 they can legally engage in certain adult activities before that age.

At 16 a young person can consent to sex, join the armed services (although they will not generally be deployed on active service until they are 18) and get married with their parent's consent. Whereas 16 year olds have traditionally been able to buy cigarettes, in October 2007 the minimum age rose to 18.

The Children Act 1989 aims to encourage parents to agree about the child's welfare in the event of separation or divorce by providing for the continuation of parental responsibility for divorced parents and by requiring the courts to refrain from making orders unless they are desirable in the child's best interests (the 'no order' principle). This approach is reinforced by the development of conciliation and mediation processes to assist parents to reach agreement.

Where there is agreement between parents they are not required to attend court in divorce proceedings in relation to the children. The court must simply be satisfied that appropriate arrangements have been made for children having received a written declaration to that effect and the divorce is granted. In cases where the court is concerned about the plans for the children it can order a welfare report but this power is very rarely used. However it is concerning that in an uncontested case there is no formal way in which children can express their views if they wish to do so.

In 2001 the Children and Family Court Advisory and Support Service (CAFCASS) was established. CAFCASS has a number of functions. In this context the most important is the provision of Child and Family Reporter to carry out conciliation and reporting functions in disputes between parents over residence and contact.

Parents making applications for residence or contact with a child may be required to attend a conciliation appointment with a mediator or child and family reporter. The purpose of the conciliation stage is to assist the parties to resolve their disputes. If this is not possible then the Court may order a report to be prepared on the matter of residence or contact. A child and family reporter involved at the conciliation plays no further part in the process and does not participate in the preparation of any reports for the court.

In addition to applications for residence and contact, which are made under section 8 of the Children Act 1989, parents can also apply for a specific issue order requiring a particular action by another parent or for a prohibited steps order to prevent a parent from taking certain steps, for example removing a child from the other parents care and control. Section 8 applications often involve the use of child and family reporters to provide the court with an objective assessment of what is in the child's best interests. Children and young people may apply to court for section 8 orders provided they can demonstrate sufficient maturity and understanding. However, the court does not have to grant a child leave, and retains a discretion to refuse an application of a competent child. (see chapter 11 for more on different order).

Welfare Principle

The concept of welfare is not defined in the Children Act 1989 but the following factors which constitute the 'welfare checklist' are used to assist the Court in its determination:

- The ascertainable wishes and feelings of the child – in light of his or her age and understanding;
- The physical, emotional and educational needs of the child;
- The likely effect of any change on the child's circumstances;
- The age, sex, background and any other characteristics which the court considers to be relevant;
- Any harm which the child has suffered or is at risk of suffering;
- How capable the child's parents (and/or any other relevant person) are of meeting the child's needs; and
- The range of powers available to the court.

The child and family reporter is also required to take the welfare checklist into account in the preparation of his or her report.

Article 8 of the ECHR – the right to respect for family life – impacts on this decision making process in that a court must be aware of the parents' right to respect for their family life. The courts have taken the view that while a balance must be struck between the competing interests of parents and children, the welfare principle continues to predominate under the Children Act 1989.

In most cases such children will not participate directly but will be represented by a children's guardian appointed by CAFCASS. Most children's guardians have worked as social workers but they are appointed to act independently and to represent the child's interests.

Contact Disputes

The question of how much contact a child should have with a non-residential parent is a difficult matter for the court to resolve to the satisfaction of the parents and the child. Under the Children Act 1989 contact is expressed as a right of the child although the ECHR has recognised it as an element of a parent's family life. In striking a balance between the competing interests the courts are guided by considerations of the child's welfare as the paramount consideration but the view in the vast majority of cases is that maintaining a relationship with both parents is in the child's best interests. Terminating direct contact between a child and a non residential parent is a rare occurrence and usually only happens where there has been violence or abuse of an extreme nature or where for other reasons the child does not wish to continue to have a relationship with his or her parents.

Education

While education is recognised as a right of the child, international and domestic human rights law have tended to focus disproportionately on the rights of parents to control the content of their children's education. For example, Article 2, Protocol 1 of the Convention states that everyone has a right to education and then goes on to say that the State has an obligation to respect the rights of parents to ensure that education and teaching of their children is in conformity with the parents' religious and philosophical convictions. The emphasis on the rights of parents as consumers in education law and policy is problematic because it dilutes the child's right to an education and it discourages acceptance of children's right to participate. The Joint Committee on Human Rights has expressed concerns about the inadequacy of recent education legislation, in light of Article 12 UNCRC.

The law governing education in England and Wales is complex not least because there is a range of different types of state maintained schools, independent (albeit state funded) schools such as Academies and City Technology Colleges, and fully independent schools . Further, the Education and Inspections Act 2006 allowed schools to become Trust (foundation) schools.

Compulsory education

Children over the age of five and under the age of 16 are of compulsory education age and they must receive full time education. Parents are required to ensure that a child receives efficient full-time education suitable to his or her age, ability and aptitude and to ensure that any special educational needs are met by attendance at school or otherwise. Parents may educate children at home or engage a private tutor, but the Local Education Authority (LEA) must be satisfied that the education is of a sufficiently high standard. If the LEA are concerned that a child is not receiving a suitable education other than at school they may serve formal notice on the parents requiring them to satisfy the LEA otherwise. Where the parents fail to do so, the LEA can serve a School Attendance Order (SAO) requiring the parents to register the child at a named school.

Parents must be given notice of the LEA's intention to serve this order and the named school must not be one from which the child has been excluded.

The SAO lasts while the child is of compulsory school age unless it is repealed by a court order. Where a parent fails to comply with the SAO s/he can be prosecuted before a Magistrates' Court and can be fined up to £1000. Where a parent knows that a child is not attending school and fails to take steps to make the child attend, the parent can be fined up to £2500 or imprisoned for not more than three months. A court which has convicted a parent for a failure to comply with a SAO can direct the LEA to apply for an Education Supervision Order. The LEA does not have to do this but it must tell the court why it has chosen not to make an application.

The purpose of an Education Supervision Order is to guide parents and children to ensure that the children receive a satisfactory education. The Department of Health has issued guidance on the use of Education Supervision Orders which last for up to one year initially, but may be extended for up to three years at a time. They cannot last beyond the point at which the child is no longer of compulsory school age.

Special Educational Needs

LEA's must make special provision for children who have learning disabilities to ensure that they are provided with education which meets their needs. The general preference is that children with special educational needs (SEN) remain in mainstream schools.

Schools have an obligation to ensure that a child's special educational needs are identified and known to those involved in teaching the child. This process is done by way of assessment and a child who has SEN is 'statemented' – a statement of the child's needs and measures which are to be taken to deal with those needs is provided. If parents are not satisfied with the eventual provisions or the nominated school, they may appeal to a

Special Educational Needs Tribunal provided that they require the assessment of the child themselves. The question of whether a child requires assessment and statementing can often be contentious in that parents may wish to have a child statemented but can encounter considerable difficulties in convincing a school to undertake this process.

Where the school refuses to statement a child the parents can appeal to the SEN tribunal. Each school is required to have a Special Education Needs Co-ordinator (SENCO) who is responsible for overseeing the provision of SEN for a child within the school.

Parenting Contracts and Orders

An LEA or school governing body can apply to the magistrates' court for a parenting order covering the parents of a child who has been excluded from school. The relevant exclusion must have been either permanent or for two fixed periods within twelve months. A parenting order requires the parent to exercise control over the child, and to attend counselling or a guidance programme. Parents who fail to keep to the terms of a parenting order are guilty of a criminal offence, and could be fined.

Parenting contracts are a new provision allowing for formal agreements between parents and the school or LEA, which codify the intended action in relation to a specific child's attendance and behaviour.

Adoption-The Adoption and Children Act 2002 (ACA 2002)

The central objective of adoption is now aimed at providing a stable and permanent future in a family for children who are being cared for by the local authority. The ACA 2002 (amended by the Children and Adoption Act 2006-see below) and also amended by the Children and Families Act 2014, introduced some significant improvements to existing adoption law. The main aim is to ensure that the welfare of the child is paramount (ACA 2002 s 1(2). Courts must apply this test when considering an adoption order. Also, the courts can dispense with the consent of existing parents if the welfare of the child requires it.

The 2002 ACA also recognises the geopolitics of family life-that for many children maintaining contact with birth parents is of the utmost importance. With this in mind, ACA s1 (4) (f) requires courts to consider:

'the relationship the child has with relatives, and with any other person in relation to whom the court or agency considers the relationship to be relevant, including:

(i)   the likelihood of any such relationship continuing and the value to the child of its doing so;

(ii)   the ability and willingness of any of the child's relatives, or of any such person to provide the child with a secure environment in which the child can develop, and otherwise to meet the child's needs;

(iii)   the wishes and feelings of any of the child's relatives, or of any such person, regarding the child.

Adoption services

Under the ACA 2002, only a local authority or a registered adoption society can provide adoption services. The latter must be registered under the National Care Standards Commission. Under s4 (1) of the act 'adoption agencies' have responsibility for selecting and assessing adopters and placing children for adoption. This includes the provision of support services, discussed below. S5 states that local authorities must prepare a clear adoption plan for the provision of services with regard to the adoption of the child. Section 109 requires the court to draw up a plan with a view to determining applications.

The Adopted Children Register And The Adoption Contact Register
The Adopted Children Register is a register of adoptions taking place in England & Wales and is kept in the General Register Office, but the Register itself is not open to public inspection or search. However, the index of the Register is available for inspection and anyone can apply on payment of a fee for a certified copy of an entry in the register relating to a child who has reached 18.

An adopted person can apply to obtain a copy of their birth certificate but the Local Authority must make the application.

The Adopted Contact Register is also a register kept at the General register office and again the register itself is not available for public inspection and search but it is possible to apply for certified copies of entries in the register. The register contains information about adopted persons who have given notice expressing a wish to make contact with their relatives and who have reached 18.

Opening up of adoption information
From December 2013, families have a greater say in selecting which child to adopt under radical new measures. Couples are able to check online which councils can best help them find a child, instead of being limited to their local authority. From 2014, families approved for adoption are also be able to browse profiles of thousands of children waiting for a new home. Access to the adoption register has previously been the preserve of social workers who decide on parents behalf which children make a good match. The progress of councils in recruiting more adopters will be overseen by a new Adoption Leadership Board.

Care plans
Where the local authority wishes to place a child for adoption, it is the duty of the local authority in all care cases to file a care plan. The care plan sets out the local authority's plans for the child's future. The local

authority may take the view that adoption is the preferred option. If this is the case, it should advise the court of the likely steps and timescales.

Adoption of children from overseas

There are rules and procedures governing the adoption of children overseas. Anyone wishing to adopt a child from overseas must apply for an eligibility certificate' from a casework team at the Department of Education. The Children and Adoption Act 2006 has introduced new regulations concerning the adoption of children overseas, see summary below.

Who can be adopted?

A person can only be adopted if he or she is under 19 years of age. The application must be made before the child is 18 years old. In practice, if a child is over 12 then removing a child from parents or foster parents may not be in the interests of the child. The local authority will usually look for other alternatives. they must not have been married or have entered into a civil partnership at any time. No application can be made in relation to a child who is under six weeks old.

Who can adopt? Sections 49-51 AC 2002

- A single person
- A person who is the partner of a parent of the person to be adopted
- A married couple
- A couple who have entered into a civil partnership
- An unmarried couple (whether heterosexual or homosexual) who are living a spartners in a stable and enduring family relationship
- A prospective adopter must be at least 21 years of age, except a natural parent of a child who must be at least 18

- They must have been habitually resident in the British Isles for at least a year
- They (or one of them if it is a joint application) must be domiciled in the British isles (or habitually resident, together with a fixed intention to live there permanently).

It has to be remembered that under s 51(3) a married person can only adopt on their own if it can be shown that their spouse cannot be found or that they are permanently separated or that their spouses mental or physical condition is such that they are incapable of making an application.

Matching parents and children

The ACA 2002 also places emphasis on the importance of religious persuasion, racial origin and cultural and linguistic background in the process of matching adoptive parents to children placed for adoption. However, under the 2014 Children and families Act this is not a requirement in England. It is recognised that perfect matching may not always be possible, in fact it will be impossible to match all the variables. In Re C (Adoption: Religious Observance (2002) a child of a mixed race background with Jewish, Irish Roman Catholic and Turkish Cypriot Muslim elements was placed for adoption with a Jewish couple. The guardian for the child issued proceedings arguing that the couple were too Jewish and that the child should be placed in a secular home. The court held that where a child's heritage was very mixed, it would rarely be possible for it all to be reflected in the identity of the adoptive home.

Regulation and review of decisions

The ACA 2002, s 45, provides for the regulation of agency decisions in respect of suitability. A system of review introduced by the Act ensures that what are called 'qualifying determinations' which are decisions that conclude that a prospective applicant is unsuitable, are subject to review. A system of review is established and decisions about suitability are subject to an independent review. Complaints can be made to the local authority.

Court orders

The two orders of the court with regard to adoption are:

- a placement order
- an adoption order
- Post-adoption contact orders

Placement order

A placement order is an order authorising a local authority to place a child for adoption where there is parental consent, or where there is no consent and consent can be dispensed with. The court can only make a placement order where the child is subject to a care order. Conditions for making a care order are met when the child has no parent or guardian and the parents have consented or their consent should be dispensed with.

If parents refuse consent the court can dispense with consent on two statutory grounds. The first ground (s52(2)(a)) is where the parent or guardian cannot be found or is incapable of giving consent. The second ground (s52(2)(b)) is where the welfare of the child requires the consent to be dispensed with.

Adoption order

Under the ACA 2002 s 46, an adoption order is made by the court on an application under s 50 or s 51 giving parental responsibility for the child to adopters. These can be made by the high court, county court or magistrates court. No order can be made without the child attending the hearing, unless special circumstances exist. An adoption order gives parental responsibility to the adopters and the child is treated as if born to the adopters in marriage.

97

Each parent/guardian must be joined as a respondent as well as the adoption agency or local authority which has care of the child. If the adoption is refused, the child must be returned to the adoption agency within seven days of the order. The court can make a short term order which gives the applicant parental responsibility for two years and not more. Conditions can be attached to the order.

Alternatives to adoption orders

The ACA 2002 s 1(6) requires the court to be satisfied that the order it makes is better than the alternative order or making no order at all. The court is required to consider all alternatives and will look to maintain links with the natural family.

Post -adoption contact orders

Section 9 of the Children and Familes Act 2014 provides for post-adoption contact orders to be made, and allows a court to prohibit contact. Such an order may be made on application by the adopters or the child, or by anyone else with the courts leave.

Adoption by step-parents

The ACA 2000, s 39, provides for adoption by partners of parents. However, it is expected that fewer stepparents will apply for adoption as a parental responsibility order can also infer parental responsibility.

Protection of Children and the Resolution of Disputes

Section 8 of the Children Act 1989 outlines the orders which can be issued by the court with respect to resolving disputes over children. These orders have become known as *Section 8 Orders*.

Notably, these orders are not granted to the local authority. They are for the resolution of family disputes and are aspects of private law.

The Children Act makes it very clear that these orders are not to be sought as the first option and that all efforts should be made to resolve problems voluntarily. Only when there has been no resolution of the matter should these Court Orders be sought, and only then if they will be of positive benefit to the child.

Originally, four different types of Order were laid down in Section 8. With the advent of the Children and Families Act 2014, these were reduced to three, Contact Orders and Residence Orders being replaced by Child Arrangements Orders:

Child Arrangements Orders
Prohibited Steps Orders
Specific Issue Orders

"*Section 8 Orders*" refer to any of the above orders, or any order varying or discharging such an order.

A "child arrangements order" gives the Court's decision in terms of an order regulating arrangements concerning with whom a child is to live, spend time or otherwise have contact and when a child is to live, spend time or otherwise have contact with any person.

A "prohibited steps order" gives the Court's decision in terms of restricting the exercise of full parental responsibility without specific consent of the court, where it is believed that this responsibility would be abused and not exercised to the benefit of the child. For instance such an order may prohibit contact with the child except by prior arrangement and under supervision, where there is concern the child may be harmed or abducted.

A "specific issue order" gives the Court's directions in answer to a disagreement that has arisen with regard to the exercising of parental responsibility for the child.

When an application is made to the court for a section 8 order the court takes into account: the nature of the proposed application; the connection the person has to the child; the disruption that could be caused to the child and, if the child is being looked after by the local authority: the local authorities plans for the child's future and the wishes of the child's parents.

Who can apply for a Child Arrangements Order (Residence Order)?

You can apply for a Child Arrangements Order (Residence) if you:

- Are the child's parent, guardian or special guardian
- Are the child's step parent, who is married to (or is a civil partner of) the child's parent and the child has lived with you as a 'child of the family'
- Are a foster carer approved by Children's Services who has had the child living with you for at least one year
- Are a grandparent, aunt, uncle, sibling or step parent and you have had the child living with you for one year
- Are anyone else and the child has been living with you for at least 3 years (in the last 5 years)
- Have the agreement of anyone who already has a Residence Order on the child; or Children's Services if the child is in care; or
- Everyone else with parental responsibility for the child.

If Social Services are involved

When family circumstances mean that a parent cannot provide a family life for their child, social care professionals are often involved. You may find that they are involved with the case because of:

- S20 Accommodation – (Residence application to avoid care proceedings/stabilise position of child)

- Care order – Grandparent(s) apply for a Child Arrangement Order for Residence as alternative to care order.
- Local Authority is considering Adoption
- Local Authority suggests Grandparent(s) apply for Child Arrangement Order for Residence after child placed with
- them under care order/accommodated
- Social Care Services feel Section 47 threshold (relating to child protection) is not met –
- Grandparent(s) don't agree. Child Arrangement Order for Residence taken out as a protective mechanism

It is important that if you are considering a Child Arrangements Order (Residence) for whatever reason that you make yourself known to social services as they by law (s23 (6) Children Act) have a duty to place child with family or friends unless not 'reasonably practicable' or consistent with the child's welfare.

At this point you can ask for a Family Group Conference (FGC). This is a family-led decision-making process in which the whole family comes together to make plans and decisions for a child who needs a plan that will keep them safe and promote their welfare. Professionals (for example social workers) are involved in setting out their key concerns which must be addressed in the plan at the start of the meeting and agreeing the plan, and help from Children's Services, in the last stage of the meeting. The family are given time to draw up a plan in private which meets the child's needs and addresses the professionals' concerns.

What Court should I contact?

There is now only one Court and that is the Single Family Court, introduced by the Children and families Act 2014. This court acts as a gatekeeper. You will now just issue a family application at your local

Family Court who will then decide which level of Judge and which Court will hear the application.

Generally speaking you should apply to the court nearest to where the child lives. However, if you are making an application about a child where there are existing proceedings about that child, you should apply to the same court which is dealing with that case.

Mediation and MIAMS

From April 22nd 2014, anyone applying to the Family Court for assistance in resolving a dispute about parenting or finances following relationship breakdown must undertake compulsory family mediation information meetings (MIAM) and prove to the court that they have done so in the application to the court. (see example at the end of this guidance.) There are some exemptions to this need to attend a MIAM including domestic violence and child abuse. Addresses below.

- National Family Mediation (NFM). http://www.nfm.org.uk or ring 0300 4000 636
- Family Mediation Council (FMC)
- www.familymediationcouncil.org.uk

If, after your MIAM, it's considered that mediation is not suitable in your case, the mediator will fill in a form – called the FM – which is now included in the C100 form (see page 19). Signed by a certified mediator, this form confirms that you have attended a MIAM. A court will then allow you to issue proceedings.

This gives the information which will be considered by the court when deciding whether to grant 'leave' to apply (as laid down in the Children Act Part II, s10 (9)).

- What sort of order you wish to apply for.
- Your relationship and personal connection to the child.

- Whether awarding you an order about where a child should live and with whom they should have contact would cause disruption to the child to the extent that they were harmed.

Where the child is 'looked after' by a Local Authority the court must also consider:

- The Local Authority's plans for the child's future.
- The wishes & feelings of the child's parents.

Different types of proceedings

The only way for private individuals to take steps to resolve disputes concerning bringing up a child is for one of them to issue proceeding under the Children's Act. Like the above orders, the Children's Act has greatly simplified dispute resolution. The only exceptions to this relate to wardship and adoption.

Under the Children's Act it is possible to apply for an order appointing a guardian of the child (s 5). An order of this type gives parental responsibility. It is also possible for an unmarried father to apply far an order that gives him parental responsibility. The main type of application possible under the Children Act however, is a section 8 order.

An application for such an order can be made in several ways, either as a "free standing application" or as part of "family proceedings" Section 8 defines "family proceedings" The list includes jurisdictions which used to have their own powers to grant orders relating to upbringing of children, for example the M.C.A. It also includes applications under part one of the Children's Act itself. It should be noted that once family proceedings have commenced, the court can make a section 8 order itself, of its own motion.

Types of applicant

In most cases, it is the parents of the child who are in dispute about its upbringing. However, others with an interest in the child's welfare may also make an application. The Children Act recognises the need for persons other than parents of a child to be able to get orders that relate to the child's upbringing:

Those entitled to apply for any s 8 order:

1. A parent or guardian of the child;
2. A person who has been granted a residence order.

Those entitled to apply for a residence or contact order:
1. A spouse or ex spouse in relation to whom the child is a child of the family;
2. A person with whom the child has lived for at least three years. This need not be continuous as long as the period does not begin more than five years, nor end more than three months before, the making of the application;
3. A person who has the consent of the person in whose favour there is a residence order, if one has been granted, the local authority if the child is in care and in any other case any other person with parental responsibility.
The factors a court must take into account when considering making an order are designed to prevent applications deemed not to be serious and also possibly injurious to the child's future well-being. They include the nature of the persons connection with a child (s 10 (9)).

Protection of Children-Local Authorities
Types of orders available
Before the Children's Act came into being, there were many types of orders available to local authorities which enabled them to offer some form of protection to children. Local authorities could, on passing a specific resolution, assume the role of parent. The Children's Act makes an

attempt to get rid of the uncertainty of the old laws. It replaced all the old laws with a new scheme. In addition, local authorities can no longer pass a parental rights resolution. No child may be taken into care without a court order.

The following orders are available:

1.Care orders (s 31);
2. Supervision orders (s 31);
3.The Education supervision order (s 36);
4.The Emergency protection order (s 44);
5.The Child assessment order (s 43).

Care orders
This is an order that commits a child into the care of a local authority. It cannot be made in favour of anyone else. The effect of a care order is that the child in question goes to live in a local authority community home, or with local authority foster parents. The legal effect is that the local authority gains parental responsibility for the child while the order is in force. A care order automatically brings to an end any residence order that exists. But if a parent or guardian has parental responsibility at the time that a care order comes into force, this continues. A care order cannot be made in respect of a child who has reached 17 (16 if married). It lasts until the age of 18.

Supervision orders
This is an order placing the child under the supervision of a local authority or probation officer. This order does not carry any parental responsibility and there is no power to take a child from his home.

A supervision order can have conditions attached to it as the court sees fit. A supervision order cannot be made in respect of a child who has reached the age of 17 (16 if married). Generally, a supervision order has a life span of one year but can be extended to two years.

Education supervision orders

This is an order placing a child under the supervision of the local education authority.

Emergency protection orders

Orders usually take time to activate. For those children requiring emergency protection the above order is issued. It is an order that empowers the local authority or NSPCC to remove a child from its home and also gives the local authority parental responsibility. Applications can be made ex-parte, without the necessity of informing or involving the child's parents or any other person. In this way, it is possible to obtain the court order very quickly indeed. The order lasts for eight days only and can be extended for a further seven days. After 72 hours, an application for its discharge can be made.

The child assessment order

This order is a new concept, the above replacing orders already in existence. Although a local authority may feel that a child is at risk there are times when it cannot gain access to the child to compile evidence. In the past the local authority could apply for a place of safety order and remove the child immediately from its home. It could also do nothing. The child assessment order has effect for seven days maximum. With such an order it is possible to remove a child from its home. There is no parental responsibility. The intention behind the order is to enable the local authority to assess the child so it can make the necessary arrangements after consideration.

Before the Children's Act came into being, it was possible to make orders giving a local authority the right to intervene in a child's life under a number of jurisdictions, some overlapping. The Children's Act is now the only jurisdiction under which a local authority may act. By section 31 (4) an application for a care order or a supervision order can be made on its own or within family proceedings as defined by section 8 (3) of the Act. Applications for education supervision orders, emergency protection orders and child assessment orders have to made alone.

Categories of applicants for orders are limited to the following:

Care orders, supervision orders and child assessment orders-only a local authority or NSPCC may apply. Education supervision orders-only a local education authority may apply. Emergency protection orders-only a local authority may apply. In place of previous powers to make different orders, the court now has intermediate powers under section 37. Where a court is dealing with family proceedings in which a question relating to the welfare of a child arises, it may direct the local authority to carry out investigations. The local authority must respond and decide what order should be applied for. If the local authority decides not to apply for an order the court cannot make it do so, although this fact must be reported to the court.

Grounds on which a court will grant an order (s 31(2))

A court has to be satisfied of the following before granting an order:
(a) that the child has suffered or is likely to suffer significant harm;
(b) that the harm or likelihood of harm is attributable to the care given to the child, or likely to be given to him if the order were not made or the child being beyond parental control. Proof of the ground in section 31(2) only entitles accoutre to grant a care or supervision order. The court does not have to grant such an order. The grounds in this section are referred to as "threshold" grounds.

In relation to education and supervision orders, the court has to be satisfied that the child is of compulsory school age and not being properly

107

educated. To obtain an emergency protection order, the local authority must demonstrate the following:

(a) a local authority must show that the enquiries are being frustrated and that access to the child is required urgently;

(b) the NSPCC must show that it has reasonable cause to suspect that the child is in danger of suffering significant harm;

(c) any other applicant must show that there is reasonable cause to believe that the child is likely to suffer significant harm if he is not removed from the home.

As with the other orders, applications for emergency protection orders are subject to section 1 of the Act. For child assessment orders, the court has to be satisfied that:

(a) the applicant has reasonable cause to suspect that the child is suffering or likely to suffer significant harm;

(b) this can only be determined by an assessment of the child's health or development;

(c) it is not likely that an assessment can be made without an order.

Again, applications for this order are subject to section 1 of the Children Act.

Parental contact

By section 34 of the Act a local authority is under a duty to allow reasonable contact between a child in care and his parents. If there is any dispute on the reasonableness of contact, the court can regulate. In limited circumstances, a local authority can refuse to allow contact for up to seven days. By section 43, if a child is to be kept away from home during the currency of the child assent order, the order must contain directions for such contact between the child and other persons as the court thinks fit.

By section 44, an applicant who is granted such an order is placed under a duty to allow reasonable contact between child and parents.

Wardship

Wardship is the means by which the family court fulfils its jurisdiction of protection of children. When a child becomes a ward of court, the court controls its upbringing by a series of orders.

The Children and Young Persons Act 2008

The Children's and Young Persons Act received royal assent in November 2008. The purpose of the Act was to reform the statutory framework for the care system by implementing the proposals in the June 2007 white paper, Care Matters: Time for Change, that require primary legislation. It includes provision in relation to private fostering, child death notification to Local Safeguarding Children's Boards and the secretary of state's powers to conduct research and applications for the discharge of emergency protection orders. The Act also amends the public law framework for safeguarding and promoting children's welfare through amendments to the services that are to be provided to support children and their families and the procedures to protect children who are at risk of suffering harm.

International Child Abduction

Section 1(2) Child Abduction Act 1984 makes it an offence for a person connected with the child to remove a child under 16 from the UK (without consent from certain specified people). Parent child abduction can take two forms: Removal without consent; Retention once consent has expired. The difference between removal and retention was clarified in the House of Lords in Re H: Re S (Abduction; Custody Rights 1991). Removal is 'when a child, which has previously been in the state of its habitual residence, is taken away across the frontier of that state'. Retention is 'where a child, which has previously been for a limited period of time outside the state of its habitual residence, is not returned on the expiry of such limited period'.

The Child Abduction Act 1984 creates a range of criminal offences to deal with the full range of potential child abductions. Section 1(1) deals with international parent-child abduction.

This states that:

- o   A person connected with a child under 16 years of age commits an offence if they take or send the child out of the United Kingdom without the appropriate consent.

A person is 'connected with a child' if they are a parent or guardian or special guardian of the child; anyone named in a child arrangements order as the person with whom the child will live or who has custody of the child; and if a child's parents were not married to each other at the time of his birth, there are reasonable grounds for believing that the man is the father of the child.

Section 1(3) defines the 'appropriate consent' in relation to a child as:

- the consent of each of the child's mother, father (if he has parental responsibility for him); a guardian; anyone who the child lives with under a child arrangements order or anyone who has custody of the child; or
- the leave of the court granted under Part 11 Children Act 1989, or the leave of any court which has awarded the custody of the child to anyone.

Section 1(4) and s 1(5) provide for defences to a s 1(1) charge.

A person does not commit an offence if he has a child arrangements order in his favour providing for the child to live with him *and* he takes or sends the child out of the UK for less than a month, unless he does so in breach of an order under Part 11 of the Children Act 1989. Section 1(5) elaborates on this.

****

Ch. 8

The Law and Divorce

Divorce law has developed over the years through legislation made by Parliament and through the build up of "precedents" or through cases decided by the courts. However, in the last thirty years there have been fundamental changes in the way society, and the law, has come to view divorce.

Modern divorce law recognizes that "Irretrievable breakdown" of a marriage should be the one and only ground for divorce. This recognition signalled a move away from the idea of "guilty parties" in divorce.

Before the introduction of the notion of irretrievable breakdown it was held that one party had to prove that the other party was guilty of destroying the marriage before divorce could be granted. The law is now much more flexible in its recognition of the breakdown of a marriage.

Since the present law was introduced, making it much easier to obtain divorce, the number of marriage breakdowns in Britain has risen significantly, with one in three couples in Britain filing for divorce. This is currently the highest rate in Europe.

There are a lot of problems associated with the law, and the role of those who make divorce law generally. The whole question of divorce law is under scrutiny, particularly the question of whether or not the law should attempt to keep marriages intact or whether it should seek to ease the transition to final separation without presenting unnecessary obstacles.

However, although we hear periodic announcements from different politicians on the importance of keeping the family unit intact, and by implication making it harder for people to divorce, the whole climate has changed over the years whereby the law seems to be the facilitator of divorce as opposed to dictating whether or not people can get a divorce.

There has also been a major shift in the law concerning children of divorcing couples. Under The Children Act of 1989 (as amended), parents in divorce proceedings are encouraged to take the initiative and take matters into their own hands, making their own decisions concerning the child's future life after divorce. The courts role has been greatly restricted.

The Child Support Act 1991 (as amended by the 1995 CSA) has also dramatically changed the role of the courts in divorce proceedings. After April 1993, maintenance applications are no longer a matter for the courts but for a new government agency, the Child Support Agency (subsumed within the Child Maintenance and Enforcement Commission) which assesses and determines applications for maintenance in accordance with a set formula. The courts will only now deal with applications for maintenance in certain circumstances.

The courts

Before looking at the law surrounding divorce in greater depth we should look briefly at the structure of the courts and how divorce law is administered.

Most divorces are handled by a branch of the County Court system known as the Divorce County Courts.

Not all county courts are able to deal with divorce, those that can are known as divorce county courts. Decisions concerning divorce cases, and subsequent orders, are made by Judges and District Judges. These people are appointed from the ranks of senior lawyers. In London, the equivalent of the divorce county court is known as the "Divorce Registry" and is based in the Royal Courts of Justice in the Strand.

The High Court

Sometimes, rarely, divorce cases need to be referred to the High Court. There are several sections of the high court-the section responsible for divorce and other similar matters is known as the Family Division. However, the majority of divorce cases will be heard in the County Courts.

Hearing your divorce case

Hearings related to divorce cases are either in "Open" court or in "Chambers". Proceedings in open court are heard in the courtroom itself. They are usually formal and members of the public are allowed to attend. However, most divorces are heard in chambers. These proceedings are private and the general public has no right to attend or listen. Only those people directly concerned with the case are allowed to attend.

Seeking a divorce – the grounds for divorce

The first question facing couples wishing to divorce is whether or not they qualify at the outset to bring proceedings, i.e., what are the ground rules.

If one or other parties wishes to file for divorce, the most basic requirement that must be fulfilled is that they should have been married for one-year minimum. They must also be "domiciled" in this country, i.e., England is regarded as their home. Alternatively, they must have been resident in England for one year before the date on which proceedings are brought.

A court can halt proceedings for divorce in England if it would be better for the case to be heard in another country. Usually, the court would try to decide which country is the most appropriate, or with which country the divorcing couple are most closely associated.

Grounds for divorce – the five facts.

As we have seen, there is only one ground for granting a divorce, that is the irretrievable breakdown of marriage. Fundamentally, this means that your marriage has broken down to such a degree that it cannot be retrieved and the only solution is to end it legally.

The person, or spouse, who requests a divorce is known as the "petitioner". the other party is known as the "respondent". Although there

114

is only one ground for divorce, the court has to be satisfied that there is clear evidence of one of the following five facts:

1. that the respondent has committed adultery and the petitioner cannot, or finds it intolerable, to live with the respondent;

2. that the respondent has behaved in such a way that you cannot reasonably be expected to live with him or her (unreasonable behaviour)

3. that the respondent has deserted you for a continuous period of two years immediately before the presentation of your petition for divorce.

4. that parties to a marriage have lived apart for more than two years prior to filing for divorce and that there is no objection or defence to filing for divorce. This is known as the "no fault" ground;

5. that parties to marriage have lived apart continuously five years prior to filing for divorce.

We should now look at each of these "five facts" in more depth.

1. Adultery

Quite simply, adultery is defined as heterosexual sex between one party to a marriage and someone else. Oddly enough, because the law states quite clearly heterosexual sex, then gay or lesbian sex cannot (in theory) constitute adultery. Adultery usually means that a "full" sexual act has been committed so therefore if there has not been penetration then this will not be seen to be adulterous.

For adultery to be proved, an admission by the respondent or evidence of adultery is usually sufficient. The co-respondent need not be named in the divorce petition. If you do mention the name of the co-respondent involved in the adultery, that person is entitled to take part in the divorce proceedings in so far as they affect them. The court will provide the co-respondent with copies of all the relevant divorce papers and he or she will have the opportunity to confirm or deny anything said about him or her in the divorce proceedings.

Proving adultery is the first step. You then have to satisfy the courts that you find it intolerable to live with the respondent any further. However, it is not essential to prove that you find it intolerable to live with the respondent because of their adultery. It may be that your marriage has been unhappy for some time and that the adulterous act has proven to be the end.

If, after you discover the respondent's adultery, you continue to live together as man and wife for a period of six months or more, you will not be able to rely on adultery as a reason for divorce. As long as the periods of living together after the adultery do not exceed six months in total, the courts will completely disregard them. This gives some room for attempts at reconciliation.

Unreasonable behaviour

Although "unreasonable behaviour" is a commonly cited fact for divorce, in practice the court has stringent criteria, which must be met before this is accepted. The law actually says that you must demonstrate that your spouse has behaved in such a way that you cannot reasonably be expected to continue to live with that person.

The court considering your case will look at the particular circumstances surrounding your situation and will then decide whether or not you should continue to tolerate your partner's behaviour within marriage.

The main principle underlying unreasonable behaviour is that it is particular to your own situation and that it cannot be seen as relative to other people's behaviour. You must prove that the behaviour of your partner has gone well beyond the kind of day-to-day irritations that many people suffer and there is real reason to grant a divorce.

Examples of such behaviour range from continuous violence and threatening or intimidating behaviour, drunkenness, sexual perversions, neglect, and imposing unreasonable restrictions on another person.

Desertion

The fact that you must prove that your spouse has deserted you for a continuous period of two years can present difficulties.

If you are seeking a divorce on the basis of desertion, then it is likely that you will need to employ a solicitor who will need to check rigorously that you comply with the often-complex requirements upon which a court will insist before granting a divorce. In the main, desertion has arisen because of other associated problems within marriage, and therefore this factor can often be joined with others when applying for a divorce

The simplest form of desertion is when one person walks out on another for no apparent reason. Desertion, however, is not just a physical separation of husband and wife. It implies that the deserting party has rejected all the normal obligations associated with marriage.

Before desertion is proven a court will need to be satisfied of two things:

1. you must demonstrate that you and your spouse have been living separately for a continuous period of two years immediately before you started the divorce proceedings. Although it is usual for separation to start when one person leaves the marital home, it can also happen whilst you are living under the same roof, but living totally separate lives.

The courts are very rigorous indeed when determining that this is the case and will need to be satisfied that your lives are indeed separate and that you can no longer go on carrying out functions jointly.

The court will disregard short periods during the separation where you may have attempted to patch up your differences. However, for example, if you attempt to reconcile six months into the initial two year period and this lasts for two months before you separate again, although the courts will not make you start again they will make you wait a further two months before they will hear your divorce. Therefore, the two years becomes two years and two months.

2. that your spouse has decided that your marriage is over-you must also be able to demonstrate that when he or she stopped living with you, your spouse viewed the marriage as ended and intended to separate from you on a permanent basis.

You will not be able to claim desertion if you consented to the separation. The court will take consent to mean that you made it clear from the outset that you consented to separation, through your words or actions.

In addition, you will not be able to claim desertion if your spouse had perfectly good reason to leave, for example he or she may have gone abroad with your full knowledge, to work or may have entered hospital for a long period.

If your spouse leaves because of your own unreasonable behaviour, then you cannot claim desertion. If you are to blame in this case, the courts will not accept desertion.

Finally, because the courts see desertion as essentially separation against your will, then if you come back together again on a permanent basis you can no longer claim desertion.

Separation for two years with consent

As with desertion, the particular circumstances in which the law looks upon you as having been separated for two years can include periods of time where you may have been under the same roof together but not functioning as a married couple. There may be short periods during this time where you have lived together, for example, an attempt at reconciliation.

However, as with desertion you will not be able to count these periods towards the two years separation. Therefore, if you have a trial reconciliation period for three months then you will have to wait two years and three months before you can apply for divorce.

The fundamental difference between desertion and separation with consent is that you would not be granted a divorce on the basis of separation if your spouse did not give his or her consent to the divorce.

The court has rigid criteria for proving that your spouse consents to the divorce. Consent is only seen as valid if your spouse has freely given it without pressure. There must also be full understanding on his or her part of what a divorce will mean and how it will affect his or her life.

The court sends a form to divorcing parties soon after initial divorce papers are filed, together with explanatory notes and it is at this point when your spouse will give consent. If your spouse will not consent to divorce and you cannot prove either desertion or adultery then you will be in the position where you will have to wait until five years separation has elapsed before you can seek a divorce.

In relation to the above, i.e., divorces granted on the basis of two years separation and consent or five years separation, the courts can exercise special powers to ensure that the financial and personal position of the respondent is protected. The courts can sometimes delay the process of divorce, or even prevent it, to make sure that there is no undue suffering or exploitation.

Five years separation
The final of the "five facts" is the fact of five years separation. If you have been separated for five or more years the courts will grant a divorce whether or not the other party agrees to it, subject to what has been said above. Again, the courts will allow for a period of attempted reconciliation up to six months and the same rules concerning length of time apply as with the other facts. Should you live together for longer than six months, the courts will demand that you start the five-year period again.

Reconciliation

As been shown, in all the provisions of the law relating to each of the five facts, which have to be demonstrated in addition to the main ground of "irretrievable breakdown", there are built in provisions for reconciliation. The law is fairly flexible when taking into account attempts at reconciling and sorting out differences.

In effect, these built in provisions allow for a period of up to six months in which both parties can make a concerted attempt at solving their problems. If these attempts are unsuccessful then their legal position vis-a-vis divorce proceedings will not be jeopardized. The reconciliation provisions apply for a period up to six months or separate periods not exceeding six months.

In addition to this, a solicitor, if you have one, will need to certify that he or she has discussed the possibility of reconciliation with you and has ensured that both parties know where to seek advice and guidance if they really wish to attempt reconciliation.

The court, if it so wishes, can also adjourn proceedings to give both parties further time to decide whether they genuinely wish to make a further effort to prolong their marriage. At the end of this book can be found names and addresses of various organizations, which can help with the process of reconciliation. The best known of these is RELATE.

Conciliation and Mediation services

There is a fundamental difference between reconciliation, and those services, which offer help, and conciliation and mediation services.

Conciliation is directed towards making parting easier to handle. The role of the conciliator is to sort out at least some of the difficulties between those who have made a definite and firm decision to obtain a divorce.

The process of conciliation can take place either out of court, or in court. In court conciliation only arises once the process of litigating for divorce has commenced. It is particularly relevant where the future of children is under discussion.

With in-court conciliation, there is usually what is known as a "pre trial review of the issues and problems which parties to a divorce are unable to settle them. Both the court welfare officer and the district judge are involved in this process.

Out of court conciliation and mediation is intended to assist both parties in reaching an agreement at a stage before they arrive in court, or approach the court. The person involved at this stage is usually always professionally trained, a social worker normally, and who will act as go between.

Both parties can also use specially trained legal personnel, lawyers to help them reach an agreement. This process is like the process of arbitration and is intended to make the formal legal proceedings less hostile and acrimonious.

Since the advent of the Family Law Act 1996, much more emphasis has been put on mediation and reconciliation, indeed this will be a central plank of the proposed new divorce process, when it finally comes into being.

Commencing proceedings

Using a solicitor-Although it makes sense to take legal advice when taking your first steps towards divorce, there is no rule that says you have to. It is important to examine the role of the solicitor, in the first instance, in order to get an idea of the advantages.

The amount of advice you will need from a solicitor will depend entirely on the circumstances of your case and the complexities involved.

Most divorces will have two fairly distinct stages - the first step of obtaining the divorce decree (divorce) and the more complicated problems of sorting out property and financial matters and making arrangements concerning children.

As with most county court procedures now, the procedure for commencing divorce and the subsequent steps up to the issuing of a decree is largely paperwork. Provided that the circumstances of your divorce are straightforward then there is no real need to consult a solicitor at all.

It is up to both parties to ascertain the complexity of the divorce before deciding to go it alone. The questions you should be asking yourselves, preferably during a face-to-face meeting, are whether or not the marriage can be ended with the minimum of problems.

If you are childless and there is no property at stake and there will be no financial complications then you should be able to proceed without a solicitor.

If, however, you own property and have children and also have life insurance policies and pension schemes etc, then you will need to try to reach agreement concerning the division of these. This is where divorce gets complicated and may entail you requesting legal advice.

The division of your assets is a matter for you but it has to be reached by agreement.

One other aspect of do-it-yourself divorce is that it can be time consuming. Some people cannot spare the valuable time involved and will be happier to leave it to a solicitor.

A solicitor will handle the whole matter for you, when instructed, from obtaining initial information you to obtaining a decree. Your main input will be to check over the necessary paperwork at each stage, as required and, in certain cases to deliver documents to the court. However, all of this will be done at the request and direction of the solicitor.

Your future arrangements

Whilst not essential to consult a solicitor, it is wise to at least get a view on future arrangements which you have negotiated. This is particularly important when it comes to future tax arrangements.

If it is necessary to ask a court to determine future arrangements, because of the inability of parties to a divorce to agree or negotiate, then a solicitor will need to take charge of the whole process. Remember, the more a solicitor does for you the more it will cost. You should both bear this in mind when beginning discussions.

An outline of divorce procedure

In undefended petitions, both spouses accept that the divorce will go ahead. In defended petitions, one party is filing a defence against the petition.

A special procedure was introduced to deal with undefended divorce petitions, primarily because of the large volume of cases presented to the courts.

At present, there is a set pattern, which you must follow if you wish to obtain a divorce:

a) the petition must be filled in
b) the petition must enclose a statement of arrangements for the children.
c) the petition must be sent to the registrar of the divorce county court.
d) there must be sufficient copies for the other parties to the divorce.
e) the respondent will then receive his or her copies from the court.
f) other parties involved will receive their copies.
g) the respondent must, on a prescribed form, acknowledge service.
h) the respondent must make clear that he or she has no intention to defend.
i) the documents are examined by a court official (the divorce registrar)
j) the divorce registrar then certifies that the facts of the case are approved.
k) the judge pronounces the decree nisi in open court.
l) the decree is made absolute on application by the petitioner.
Each of the above steps will be discussed briefly below.

The preparation of the divorce petition.

Either you or your solicitor will prepare the divorce petition. This document can be obtained from HMSO or a sample can be obtained from the county court and will form the basis of your claim for a divorce.

On this form you will record details of your marriage and your children and the grounds on which you are seeking a divorce. You will also list the claims that you are asking the court to consider. This part is particularly important. For example you may wish the court to consider financial matters for you.

Normally, you would include your address on the form but you can make application to the court to leave out your address if this poses any danger to you.

It is of the utmost importance that you take care at this stage because you are asking the court to make a very important decision on the basis of information given. You should avoid exaggerating the truth.

The statement of arrangements

If there are children involved you must fill in another document known simply as "statement of arrangements for children" This sets out the arrangements you intend to make for children once the divorce is granted.
A child, for the purposes of the court is any child who is a child of both parties, an adopted child, or any other child who has been treated by both as part of your family. This does not include children boarded out by local authorities or social services or other voluntary organizations.

Although the courts are not generally concerned with the welfare of adult children (over 16) you will be required to give details of children under 18 who are still receiving instruction at an educational establishment or undergoing other training such as for trade or profession.

The information required for the statement of arrangements will be:

a) where the children will live after divorce

b) who else will be residing there

c) who will look after them

d) where they are to be educated

e) what financial arrangements have been proposed for them

f) what arrangements have been made for the other parent to see them

g) whether they have any illness or disability

i) whether they are under the care or supervision of a person or organization (i.e. social services)

When you have completed this form your spouse should be in agreement. If she or he is not then there will be an opportunity at a later stage to make alternative proposals to the court.

Filing the papers with the court

The court office requires the following to commence proceedings:

a) the completed divorce petition (copy for spouse)

b) Completed statement of arrangements if appropriate, plus copy for spouse

c) a copy of your marriage certificate

d) In certain cases a fee if you are not receiving help under the legal help scheme

e) Once received in court the case will be given a reference number.

Serving the papers

Once the petition has been received by the courts the court office will then send a copy plus copy of statement of arrangements to the respondent. This is known as "serving" the documents on the respondent. He or she will also receive two other documents from the court-the "acknowledgement of service" and the "notice of proceedings".

The notice of proceedings informs the respondent that divorce proceedings have been commenced against him or her and that person must acknowledge service within eight days. There are further instructions concerning seeking legal help or filling in acknowledgement personally.

This document, the acknowledgement of service, is self explanatory and is designed in question and answer form. It is designed to ensure the court that the respondent has received the papers and is fully aware of impending divorce proceedings against them. The court will not proceed with the case until it has received this information.

If you have commenced proceedings on the ground of adultery then the third party, who is known as the co-respondent is entitled to be notified of the divorce proceedings.

Non-defence of divorce proceedings

Where the respondent does not wish to defend proceedings, the next steps should be quite straightforward. The court will send either you or your solicitor a copy of the completed acknowledgement of service together with copies of two more forms known as "request for directions for trial (special procedure) and the "affidavit of evidence (special procedure) The special procedure indicates that the divorce process will be streamlined. Before, all petitioners seeking a divorce had to go to court and give evidence before a judge. This is no longer necessary. Like many county court procedures the route is now simplified and quicker.

The affidavit of evidence, like all affidavits, confirms that what you have said in your petition is true. You will need to "take an oath" in front of a solicitor which is called "swearing" the affidavit. Any questions concerning the truth later could ultimately, if it is discovered that you have lied, lead to contempt of court.

The "request for directions for trial" is a basic form requesting the court to proceed with your case. Both documents, the affidavit and the request for directions are then returned to court. The case is then examined by an official of the court who will either declare that the facts of the case are proven, or otherwise. If the district judge is happy with the case he or she will issue a certificate that you are entitled too a decree of divorce. Any claims for costs will also be considered at this stage.

When a certificate has been issued, a date will be fixed for decree nisi to be pronounced in open court by judge or district judge. You will be informed of this date but you need not attend court. However, if there is a dispute over costs you will need to attend and the matter will be dealt with by the judge. Both the respondent and petitioner are then sent a copy of the decree nisi by the court. However, you have not yet reached the stage of being finally divorced. It is only when your divorce has been made absolute at a later stage that you will be free to remarry if you wish. A decree absolute follows approximately six weeks after decree nisi.

If the district judge is not satisfied that you should be granted a divorce, then you will either be asked to produce further evidence or the matter will be sent for trial. This rarely happens.

You may be entitled to legal aid if this happens. This is dependent on your income and you should seek advice. If you are refused a divorce, and you have been handling the case yourself then you will most certainly need to go and see a solicitor.

Defence of divorce

If the respondent or co-respondent has returned the papers stating that he or she intends to defend the petition, your next move will be very much dependent on whether an "answer" setting out the defence has been filed. The respondent has 29 days to file a reply.

If a defence has been filed, then the special procedure designed to speed up the process can no longer be used. In this case it is advisable to see a solicitor. There will eventually be a date given for a hearing in court at which both the petitioner and respondent will be expected to attend.

Evidence will be given to the judge who will then have to decide if a divorce should be granted. Legal aid would almost certainly be available and the whole process, depending on the defence can be quite lengthy.

If you are the respondent and you feel that you wish to defend the petition you will almost certainly need to see a solicitor and take advice. In general, undefended straightforward cases, particularly where there are no children involved, can be done on a do-it-yourself basis. Anything more complicated will mean that you will probably need to see a solicitor.

If any other problems arise, such as the respondent either failing or refusing to return acknowledgement of service, proceedings will be delayed whilst a visit by a court official is made. This visit is to ascertain and provide evidence of service.

If the respondent cannot be traced, a request can be made to the court for the petition to be heard anyway. Again, this will result in delay.

****

Ch. 9

Civil Partnerships

A Civil partnership is a legal relationship, which can be registered by two people of the same sex. Same-sex couples, within a civil partnership can obtain legal recognition for their relationship and can obtain the same benefits generally as married couples.

Civil partnerships came into force on 5th December 2005. The first civil partnerships registered in England and Wales took place on 21st December 2005. Civil partners will be treated the same as married couples in many areas, including:

- Tax, including inheritance tax
- Employment benefits
- Most state and occupational pension benefits
- Income related benefits, tax credits and child support
- Maintenance for partner and children
- Ability to apply for parental responsibility for a civil partners child
- Inheritance of a tenancy agreement
- Recognition under intestacy rules
- Access to fatal accidents compensation
- Protection from domestic violence
- Recognition for immigration and nationality purposes

The registration of a civil partnership

Two people may register a civil partnership provided they are of the same sex, not already in a civil partnership or legally married, not closely related and both over 1 although consent of a parent or guardian must be obtained if either of them are under 18.

Registering a civil partnership is a secular procedure and is carried out by the registration service, which is responsible for the registration of births, deaths and marriages. A civil partnership registration is carried out under what is termed a standard procedure, which can be varied to take into account housebound people or people who are ill and are not expected to recover.

The standard procedure for registering a civil partnership

A couple wishing to register a civil partnership just have to decide the date they want to register and where they want the registration to take place. The formal process for registering consists of two main stages-the giving of a notice of intention to register and then the registration of the civil partnership itself.

The first stage, the giving of notice is a legal requirement and both partners have to do this at a register office in the area of a local authority where they live, even if they intend to register elsewhere. The notice contains the names, age, marital or civil partnership status, address, occupation, nationality and intended venue for the civil partnership. It is a criminal offence to give false information. If one of the partners is a non-EAA citizen and subject to immigration controls (see later) there are additional requirements to be fulfilled. Once the notice has been given it is displayed at the relevant register office for 15 days. This provided an opportunity for objections to be made. The civil partnership cannot be registered until after 15 clear days have elapsed from the date of the second person gives notice.

Each partner needs to give notice in the area that they have lived for at least seven days. If the couple live in different areas then each will post a notice in their own relevant area. When giving notice they will be asked where they wish the civil partnership to take place.

Residency requirements for a civil partnerships

A couple can register a civil partnership in England and Wales as long as they have both lived in a registration district in England and Wales for at least seven days immediately before giving notice. If one person lives in Scotland and the other lives in England or Wales, the person living in Scotland may give notice there. Officers, sailors or marines on board a Royal Navy ship at sea can give notice to the captain or other commanding officer, providing they are going to register with someone who is resident in England and Wales. Service personnel based outside England and Wales have to fulfil the above residence requirements.

Documentary evidence of name, age and nationality will need to be shown. Passports and birth certificates are the main documents required. Proof of address will be required. If either partner has been married or in a civil partnership before evidence of divorce or dissolution will be required. If either partner is subject to immigration control a document showing entry clearance granted to form a civil partnership will need to be shown, along with a home office certificate of approval and indefinite leave to remain in the UK.

Civil partnership registration

A civil partnership registration can take place in any register office in England and Wales or at any venue that has been approved to hold a civil partnership. Approved premises include stately homes and other prestigious buildings including hotels and restaurants. From 5tn December 2005, any venue that has approval for civil marriage will automatically be approved for civil partnerships. A civil partnership cannot be registered on religious premises. A civil partnership can only be registered between the hours of 8am to 6pm unless one person is seriously ill and is not expected to recover.

A civil partnership is legally registered once the couple have signed the legal document, known as a civil partnership schedule, in the presence of a registrar and two witnesses. On the day, two witnesses will be required. If they wish to do so, the couple will be able to speak to each other the words contained in the schedule:

' I declare that I know of no legal reason why we may not register as each other's civil partner. I understand that on signing this document we will be forming a civil partnership with each other'

No religious service may take place, as the process of forming a civil partnership is entirely secular. A ceremony can be arranged to accompany the actual registration. This ceremony can take place at any venue as long as it is approved.

Costs of registering a civil partnership
The costs here are applicable to 2016/17. Like all other costs they will change from year to year and the current costs should always be ascertained by contacting your local register office.
The current costs are as follows:

- * Giving notice of intention to register   £35 each person
- * Registration at Register Office   £40

Registration at an approved premises-in this case the cost for attendance by a civil partnership registrar is set by the registration authority in question. A further charge may also be made by the owner for use of the building,

- Cost of civil partnership certificate on the day of registration £3.50

- Further copies of the civil partnership certificate £7

The General Register Office website www.grogov.uk has a search facility if you need to find a local register office or an office any where in the UK.

Changing names
After registering a civil partnership, one partner might want to change their surname to that of their partner. Government departments and agencies will accept civil partnership certificates as evidence for changing surnames. Other private institutions may want a different form of evidence. It is up to the individual to check with the various organisations if they wish to change their surname.

Special circumstances
Variations to the standard procedure can be made in certain circumstances. If a partner is seriously ill and is not expected to recover then a civil partnership can be registered at any time. The 15-day waiting period will not apply. A certificate will need to be provided from a doctor stating that a person is not expected to recover and cannot be moved to a place where civil partnerships take place and that they understand the nature and purpose of signing the Registrar Generals licence.

Housebound people
If one partner is housebound there are special procedures to allow them to register a civil partnership at home. A statement has to be signed, made by a doctor, confirming that this is the case and that the condition is likely to continue for the next three months. The statement must have been made no more than 14 days before notice being given and must be made on a standard form provided by the register office. The normal 15-day period will apply between giving notice and the civil partnership registration.

Detained people

There are special procedures to allow a couple to register a civil partnership at a place where one of them is detained in a hospital or prison. The couple has to provide a statement, made by the prison governor or responsible person confirming that the place where a person is detained can be named in the notice of proposed civil partnership as the place where the registration is to take place. This statement must have been made no more than 21 days prior to notice being given. The normal 15 day waiting period applies.

Gender change

The Gender Recognition Act 2004 enables transsexual people to change their legal gender by obtaining a full Gender Recognition Certificate. Where a transsexual person is married, they cannot obtain a full Gender Recognition Certificate without first ending their existing marriage. However, if they and their former spouse then wish to form a civil partnership with one another without delay, they can do so as soon as the full Gender Recognition Certificate has been issued. In those circumstances, they give notice and register on the same day. More information is available about the process of changing gender on www.grp.gro.uk

Immigration requirements for people subject to immigration controls

The civil partnerships provisions for people subject to immigration control are exactly the same as those in place for marriage. These apply if one partner is a non-EAA (European Immigration Area) citizen and is subject to immigration control, for example in the UK on a visa.

People subject to immigration control who want to give notice of a civil partnership need to do so at a register office designated for this purpose. They are required to produce one of the following as part of that notice:

- Entry clearance granted to form a civil partnership
- A Home Office certificate of approval
- Indefinite leave to remain in the UK.

Registrars are required to report any civil partnerships to the immigration service if they have any suspicions.

Application for leave to remain

Civil partners of British citizens and people settled here can apply for an initial period of two years leave to remain in the UK. If they are still together at the end of that period they can apply for indefinite leave to remain.

Work permit holders and students

Civil partners of people with temporary leave to remain in the UK, such as students and work permit holders, can apply for leave along with their civil partners.

A list of Register Offices for people subject to immigration control, can be found at www.ind.homeoffice.gov.uk or phone 0845 010 5200.

Civil partnership registration for two non-EAA citizens

Two non-EAA citizens can register a civil partnership together in the UK as long as they have entry clearance for the purpose of doing so and have resided in the registration district for at least seven days before giving notice. Registering a civil partnership doesn't affect their immigration status.

Registering civil partnerships abroad

If couples wish to register a civil partnership abroad they should contact the Embassy or High Commission in the country concerned. Couples may be asked to obtain a certificate of no impediment.

It may be possible for couples to register at a UK consulate in another country if one of them is a UK national. However, UK consulates will not register civil partnerships if the host country objects or if civil unions or same sex marriage is available in that country.

Armed Forces

Members of the Armed Forces can register civil partnerships overseas in those areas where a Servicing Registering Officer is able to offer this service.

Overseas relationships

It may be the case that a couple has formed a civil union, registered partnership, domestic partnership or same-sex marriage abroad. Couples in those kind of relationships can automatically be recognised in the UK as civil partners without having to register again provided conditions set out in sections 212 to 218 of the Civil Partnership Act are met.

- The legislation defines an overseas relationship that can be treated as a civil partnership ion the UK as one that is either specified in Schedule 20 to the Civil Partnership Act or one which meets general conditions in the Act and certain other conditions. Schedule 20 of the Act lists countries and relationships that are recognised.

A couple who have formed a relationship recognised in one of those countries can be recognised in the UK as civil partners if they are of the same sex, the relationship has been registered with a responsible body in that country, the country were eligible to enter into a civil relationship in that country and all procedural requirements have been fulfilled.

For foreign relationships in countries not listed in Schedule 20 a couple who have formed a relationship can still be recognised as civil partners if the foreign relationship meets the general conditions set out in the Civil Partnerships Act.

To find out which foreign relationships are contained within Schedule 20, which is revised periodically, go to www.homeoffice.gov.uk where you will be directed to the equalities unit.

Dissolution of relationships formed abroad

Where a couple have formed an overseas relationship and that relationship is treated as a civil partnership in the UK, they may be able to obtain a dissolution, annulment or legal separation here. Legal advice should be sought in this matter.

Family relationships

The law now recognises the role of both civil partners in respect of a child living in their household.

Adoption

Under the Adoption and Children Act 2002, which came into force on 30th December 2005, civil partners may apply jointly to adopt a child.

Parental responsibility

Under the Adoption and Children Act 2002, a person will also be able to acquire parental responsibility for the child of their civil partner. They can do this with the agreement of their civil partner. If the childs other parent also has parental responsibility, both parents must agree. Parental responsibility can also be acquired on application to the court. Civil partners will have a duty to provide maintenance for each other and any children of the civil partnership.

Social security, tax credits and child support

Entering into a civil partnership will affect entitlements to the benefits and tax credits a person may be receiving. From 5th December 2005, the income of a civil partner has been taken into account when calculating entitlement to income related benefits. These benefits include income support, income based job seekers allowance, pension credit, housing benefit and council tax benefit.

From 5th December the income of a civil partner has been taken into account when calculating entitlement to child and working tax credits. The Tax Credit Line on 0345 300 3900 can offer further advice.

Child support

From 5th December 2005, civil partners who are parents will be treated in the same way as married partners for Child Support. Also, parents who are living with a same sex partner even where they have not formed a civil partnership will be treated in the same way as parents who live together with an opposite sex partner but who are not married.

For further information contact Child Support Solutions on 03456 588683

Pensions

Survivor benefits in occupational and personal pension schemes. Surviving civil partners will be entitled to a pension based on accrued pension right. New rules for civil partners mean that a surviving partner will benefit from a survivors pension based on the contracted out pension rights accrued by their deceased partner from 1988 to the date of retirement or death if this occurs before retirement. This new rule applies to all contracted out private pension schemes.

State pensions

From 5th December 2005, civil partners have enjoyed most of the same state pension rights as husbands and they are treated the same as husbands and wives after 2010 when the treatment of men and women will be equalised. For more information concerning pensions contact the Pensions Advisory Service on 0300 123 1047.

Tax

From 5th December 2005, civil partners have been treated the same as married couples for tax purposes. Information is available from a local tax office and the HMRC website www.hmrc.gov.uk

Employment rights

Employers are required to treat both married partners and civil partners in the same way. The Employment Equality (Sexual Orientation) Regulations 2003 have been amended to ensure that civil partners receive the same treatment and can bring a claim for sexual orientation discrimination if this is not the case. Other areas where changes are made include flexible working, where a civil partner of a child under six or disabled child under 18 will be able to take advantage of flexible working arrangements. Paternity and adoption leave will now be the right of civil partners.

Wills

Like all people, couples or not, making a will is the most sensible way of ensuring equitable disposal of your assets in accordance with your wishes. The most valuable asset is usually a home and this will automatically vest in a civil partner after death of the other partner, whether or not a will expressly states this. All other property belonging to one of the civil partners will be disposed of according to the will.

If a person has a will and then registers a civil partnership it will be revoked automatically unless it expressly states otherwise.

If a person dies without making a will there are special legal rules which determine how the estate of the deceased should be shared amongst that persons relatives. Under the new law, if a civil partner dies intestate then his or her civil partner can receive a maximum of £200,000 from the estate and a half share of the amount that is left. If the deceased had children then the amount which the surviving civil partner automatically receives is £125,000 and a half share of the rest.

An application to the court can be made if a surviving civil partner feels that the will doesn't make adequate provision for them.

Life assurance

Civil partners can hold life insurance on their partner's life on the same basis as a married person. In the event of an accident caused by negligence of another then the civil partner can claim compensation and can claim bereavement damages, currently £10,000. Similarly, someone living with the deceased as though they had been in a civil partnership for two years prior to date of death will also be entitled to claim compensation as a dependant.

Tenancy rights

The general effect of the Civil Partnerships act has been to give the same rights to civil partners as married couples. The Act also equalises the rights of same sex couples who are living together as if they were civil partners and their families with those of unmarried opposite sex couples.

Private sector tenants

The same sex partner of an assured tenant or assured shorthold tenant will have the same rights of succession to a tenancy as those tenants of local authority or registered social landlords.

Dissolution of a civil partnership

A civil partnership ends only on the death of one of the civil partners, or on the dissolution of the partnership or a nullity odder or a presumption of death order by the court.

The usual route is for one of the partners to seek a dissolution order to terminate the civil partnership. Other options are available. If one party, for example, did not validly consent as a result of duress, mistake or unsoundness of mind, then a nullity order may be sought from the court. Or of both civil partners do not wish to terminate the partnership one f them may ask the court for a separation order.

The dissolution process

Whoever decides to end the civil partnership should seek legal advice. The case will usually be dealt with by a civil partnership proceedings county court, although complex cases will be referred to the high court.

To end a civil partnership the applicant (petitioner) must prove to the court that the civil partnership has irretrievably broken down. Proof of an irretrievable breakdown is based on the following:

- Unreasonable behaviour by both other civil partner
- Separation for two years with the consent of the other civil partner
- Separation for five years without the consent of the other civil partner
- If the other civil partner has deserted the applicant for a period of two years or more.

Nullity

In exceptional circumstances one party to a civil partnership may decide to seek a court order (a 'Nullity' order) to annul the civil partnership.

Separation

The grounds on which a separation order may be sought are exactly the same as those for a dissolution order. Te end result is different, as a person whose civil partnership has been dissolved is free to marry or form a new partnership whereas a person who has separated remains a civil partner.

Property and financial arrangements

If a civil partnership is ending or if the couple are \separating, they will need to decide what happens to any property belonging to them. If they agree on a division they can ask the court to approve the agreement. If they cannot agree they can ask the court to decide. The court has power to make a range of orders in relation to property and other assets including income:

- The court can make an order that one civil partner pay maintenance to the other either for the benefit of the civil partner or for the benefit of any children of the relationship. These orders are known as financial provision orders.
- The court can make an order which will adjust the property rights of the civil partners as regards to property and other assets which they own, either together or separately. This may, for example, mean ordering the transfer and ownership of property from one civil partner to another for that persons benefit or the benefit of any children (known as property adjustment orders)
- The court can make an order in relation to the future pension entitlement of one of the civil partners in favour of the other. This order can relate to occupational pensions, personal pensions and other annuities (known as pension sharing orders)

Financial provision orders for maintenance can be made before a civil partnership has been ended or as separation order granted by the court.

142

Property adjustment and pension sharing orders only take legal effect once dissolution, separation or nullity order has been made by the court.

Even if the couple have been able to agree on maintenance and other property issues they should seek professional advice on such issued. In most cases the solicitor dealing with the end of the civil partnership will be able to provide appropriate advice.

Care of children

Agreeing arrangements for the care of any children should be the first priority of couples who are ending their civil partnershi8ps or choosing to live apart through separation.

If a couple decide to end the civil [partnership the court will want to ensure that both partners are\ happy with the arrangements for looking after children. If a couple are unable to agree the court will decide for them, or may do so, as part of the dissolution proceedings.

****

Ch.10

Marriage (Same Sex Couples) Act 2013

The Marriage (same Sex Couples) Act 2013

The Marriage (Same Sex Couples) Act 2013 came into force on 17 July 2013 and allows same-sex couples the same right to marry as opposite-sex couples. Civil partnerships can also be converted to marriage. Ceremonies will be able to take place in any civil venue and religious organisations will have the opportunity to "opt in" to performing religious same-sex marriages. However, the Church of England and the Church in Wales are specifically prevented by the legislation from conducting same-sex marriages.

The new Act remains separate from the Marriage Act 1949, which allows opposite-sex couples to marry, although the provisions are largely the same and afford married same-sex couples the same legal status as married opposite-sex couples. The term "marriage" and "married couple" is now extended to include same-sex couples.

However, there are some differences between the provisions for annulment and divorce for same-sex marriages in the Marriage (Same Sex Couples) Act and those provided for same-sex couples in the Matrimonial Causes Act 1973.

One of the grounds upon which an opposite-sex marriage may be annulled is for non-consummation due to the incapacity of either party to consummate it or the wilful refusal of the other spouse to consummate it. Although a same-sex marriage may also be annulled, the non-consummation ground does not apply.

In obtaining a divorce, an opposite-sex spouse may rely on the adultery of the other to prove that the marriage has irretrievably broken down. The definition of adultery is *"voluntary sexual intercourse between two persons of the opposite sex, of whom one or both is married but who are not married to each other"*. The Marriage (Same Sex Couples) Act has amended the Matrimonial Causes Act to add that *"only conduct between the respondent and a person of the opposite sex may constitute adultery for the purposes of this section."* A same-sex spouse would therefore be unable to obtain a divorce based on adultery (although any alleged infidelity with another person of the same sex could be used as evidence of unreasonable behaviour in support of a divorce application).

The new legislation also makes some alterations to the Gender Reassignment Act 2004, as it will now be possible for a transgender person to remain married after changing their gender, provided their spouse agrees.

Previously, an application for a Gender Recognition Certificate (to be recognised legally as a person of the opposite sex) had to include a statutory declaration as to whether or not the applicant was married or in a civil partnership, as obtaining the Gender Recognition Certificate (GRC) would have the effect of making the marriage or civil partnership void.

Following the new legislation, a married person applying for a GRC may remain married if their spouse consents. Applications for GRCs will now have to include a statutory declaration stating where the marriage took place together with a statutory declaration from the applicant's spouse to say that they consent to the marriage continuing after the issue of a full GRC. If the spouse does not consent, a statutory declaration will need to be made by the applicant to say that their spouse has not made a statutory declaration consenting to the marriage continuing, and the marriage will be made void.

A same-sex marriage remains distinct from a civil partnership, although couples who have previously entered into a civil partnership will be able to convert it into a marriage by way of an application. The resulting marriage will then be treated as having begun on the date of the civil partnership. Details of the procedure are still to be finalised before the law is implemented.

Civil partnerships currently remain available only to opposite-sex couples but the Government has indicated that it will review this in the near future. A recent consultation found that 61% of respondents supported civil partnerships being made available to same-sex couples as well as opposite-sex couples. Similar provisions are in force in several European countries including France and The Netherlands, where the majority of couples opting for civil partnerships are opposite-sex.

****

Ch. 11

Bereavement and the Law

Death and the Registration Of Death

If you suspect a person is dead, the first thing that you should do is to tell a doctor. There may be some doubt as to whether the person has died. In all cases, call a doctor or phone the ambulance service. Ask whether the doctor is going to attend. If the death of a person has been expected, then it may not be immediately necessary for a doctor to attend late at night, the next morning will do.

If the doctor does not intend to come, for reasons made very clear, then you need to ask for permission for a funeral director to remove the body. If a decision has been made that the funeral will be a cremation, the doctor will need to know as special papers will need to be drawn up which will involve an inspection, separately, by two doctors. If you intend to keep a body at home prior to such an inspection, which can be carried out in a funeral parlour, then it will be necessary to keep the room at a cool temperature.

Laying out a body

This is the first stage in preparing a body for burial or cremation. In hospital this is called the "last offices" and if carried out by a funeral director it is termed the "first office", denoting either the first or last contact. The body is washed and tidied up, eyelids closed and jaw closed. Hair is tidied, arms and legs And Hair usually grows for sometime after a death so therefore will need shaving. If a funeral director is laying out a body then a gown or everyday clothes will be applied.

Although laying out and general preparation can be carried out at home, and a funeral director can also provide a service in the home it is usual to allow the body to be taken away to a funeral parlor. An occurrence after death is Rigor Mortis, which is a stiffening of the muscles. This begins normally six hours after death and takes effect all over the body within 24 hours, after which it usually begins to wear off. In addition, about half an hour after death parts of the dead persons skin will begin to show dark patches. This activity is called hypostasis and is due to settlement of the blood in the body due to gravity.

Police involvement

In certain circumstances it may be necessary to call the police if a persons death is not due to natural circumstances. It could be that a death is the result of murder or other suspicious circumstance. It is very important not to touch anything in the room as you may disturb vital evidence. The police will take statements from anyone with the person before death. There may at times be difficulty in identifying a dead body and the police have a specific procedure in this case.

Certificate of cause of death

In the United Kingdom, every death must be recorded in the local registrar's office within five days. The Registrar will always require a certificate as to the cause of death. If the cause of death is known then the doctor attending on death will provide the certificate, which states cause, when last seen alive and whether or not any doctor has seen the body since death occurred. This certificate will be given to the family. No charge is usually made.

If the doctor concerned is uncertain about the cause of death or has not seen the body for 14 days after death then a certificate cannot be issued and the coroners office is informed. The body is taken to the coroner's mortuary and a post mortem may or may not be carried out.

The Coroner

A coroner is a qualified doctor or solicitor and is paid by the local authority. The coroner is independent of both local and central government and is responsible only to the Crown. The coroner is assisted by the coroner's officer, usually a police officer. The coroner's office has contact with the public.

When a death occurs which is not due to natural causes it must be reported to the coroner. If the deceased died of natural causes but was not seen by a doctor for a significant time before death or after death then the coroner must be reported. The deceased person's doctor will be contacted and cause of death and circumstances ascertained. If satisfied the coroner will cease involvement and issue a certificate and the family can then register the death normally.

In any cases where the doctor is uncertain as to the cause of the death then the coroner must be notified. Death resulting from industrial disease, which has given rise to compensation, must be reported to the coroner. In addition, death arising from military service must be reported, in some but not all cases. Other circumstances in which death has arisen which must be reported are:

- If the death was suspicious
- Was sudden or unexplained
- Due to neglect, i.e., poisoning, drugs etc
- Caused directly or indirectly by accident
- Suicide
- In prison or police custody
- During surgery or before recovering from the effects of anesthetic.

When a death is reported to a coroner, and an investigation is decided upon then a death cannot be registered until enquiries are complete. There will usually be a post mortem. If death is shown to be from natural causes then the family will be notified and the death can be registered normally.

The family of the deceased do not have to be consulted or asked about carrying out a post mortem. If the law requires it then the coroner has to proceed. However, if a family or individual objects they can register that objection with the coroner who has to listen and give reasons for a post mortem. If there are still objections there is the right of appeal to the High Court. This will delay disposal of the body The coroner has no duty to inform the next of kin about findings of a post mortem.

After the post mortem, and a coroner's report made to the relevant authorities, the body becomes the responsibility of the family.

The coroner is obliged to hold an inquest into every violent and unnatural death and also death whilst in prison. The inquest is open to the public and can take the form of a trial, with witnesses called. The office of the coroner is a powerful office and the intention is to ensure that death was natural and not due to violent or other unnatural means.

After the inquest is over then the death can be registered in the normal way.

Information concerning death, including the handing in of a certificate or the informing of the registrar of an extended period without certificate due to post mortem or other examination, can be given at any registrar's office (In England and Wales). This will then be passed on to the appropriate district or sub office.

Registration of death

As stated, in England, Wales and Northern Ireland a death should be registered within five days of occurrence. Registration can be delayed for up to another nine days if the registrar receives written confirmation that a doctor has signed a medical certificate of cause of death.

The medical certificate must be presented at the register office in the sub-district where the death occurred. The person registering death must decide how many copies of the death certificate is needed and pay for them at the office. Payment must be by cheque, not cash or credit card. If the death certificate is to be sent to someone else then the details must be given to the registrar. It is possible at this stage for what is known as the "green certificate" authorising burial or cremation to be sent to the funeral director carrying out the funeral arrangements.

Names addresses and phone numbers of local registrars can be found in doctors surgeries, libraries etc.

Registrar's requirements

Registrar's information is contained on a part of a medical certificate issued by the doctor. This part is entitled "notice to informant" and lists:

- The date and place of death
- The full name, including maiden name if appropriate of the deceased
- Date of birth
- Occupation
- Occupation of the husband if deceased was a married woman or widow
- Address
- Whether deceased was in receipt of pension or allowance from public funds
- If the deceased was married, the date of birth of the surviving partner

The form also states that the deceased's medical card should be given to the registrar.

The other side of this particular form gives details of who is qualified to inform the registrar of a death. If the death occurs in a house or any other public building, the following can inform a registrar of a death:

- A relative of the deceased who was present at the death
- A relative who was present during the last illness
- A relative of the deceased who was not present at the death or

151

during the last illness but who lives in the district or sub-district where the death occurred

- A person who is not a relative but who was present at the time of death
- The occupier of the building where the death occurred, if aware of the details of death
- Any inmate of the building where the death occurred, if aware of the details of death
- The person causing the disposal of the body, meaning the person accepting responsibility for arranging the funeral, but not the funeral director, who cannot register the death

The above are in order of preference. If a person has been found dead elsewhere, the following are qualified to register the death:

- Any relative of the dead person able to provide the registrar with the required details
- Any person present at time of death
- The person who found the body
- The person in charge of the body (which will be the police if the body cannot be identified)
- The person accepting responsibility for arranging the funeral

Only a person qualified under the law can inform of the death. If the registrar considers that the cause of death supplied on the medical certificate is inadequate, or the death should have been reported to the coroner, the registrar must inform the coroner and wait for written authority to proceed before continuing with registration.

In cases where a coroner's inquest has been held, the coroner will act as the person informing death.

Registering a stillbirth

A stillborn child is a child born after the 24th week of pregnancy which did not at any time after being completely delivered from its mother breathe or show any signs of life.

In the case of a stillbirth, both birth and death need to be registered. This is a single operation, which must be achieved within 42 days. Those qualified to register a stillbirth are:

- The mother
- The father if the child would have been legitimate had it been born alive
- The occupier of the house or other premises in which the stillbirth occurred
- A person who was present at the stillbirth or who found the stillborn child.

If a doctor was present during stillbirth that person can issue a certificate of stillbirth stating the cause of stillbirth and the duration of pregnancy. A certified midwife can also issue the certificate if a doctor was not present. If no doctor or midwife was present a parent or other qualified person can make a declaration on form 35, available from the registrar of births and deaths, saying that to the best of knowledge the child was stillborn.

If there is any doubt as to whether the child was born alive or dead then details must be given to the coroner who may then order a post mortem or inquest into the death, following which a certificate can be issued.

Loss of foetus within 24 weeks is not considered to be a stillbirth but is categorised as a miscarriage. If the mother was in hospital at the time of the miscarriage, the hospital may offer to dispose of the remains, or to arrange for disposal. But if the parent(s) would like these buried or cremated in the usual way, it should be possible to arrange this with a cemetery or crematorium, provided a medical certificate is completed.

A lot of funeral directors will give their services free of charge on such occasions, although there may be a fee for crematoria that is incurred on behalf of clients.

Some hospitals offer reverent disposal of stillborn and miscarried children, which often involves a simple ceremony led by a chaplain. In such cases there may be no ashes for subsequent burial or scattering.

Death in a hospital

There is a slight difference to the procedures up to the time of registration if a death is in hospital.

The relatives or next of kin are informed of the death by the hospital staff. If death was unexpected, for example, the result of an operation or accident, the coroner will be involved. Usually, all deaths occurring within 24 hours of an operation will be reported to the coroner. The coroner must by law be informed of all deaths under suspicious circumstances, or death due to medical mishap, industrial disease, violence, neglect, abortion or any kind of poisoning. If the person who died was not already an in-patient in a hospital then a member of the family may be asked to identify the body.

In cases where the coroner is involved it will not be possible to issue a medical certificate of the cause of death, but in other cases this is usually issued by the hospital doctor and given to the next of kin. If the person died before the hospital doctor had the chance to diagnose the cause, then the deceased patient's own doctor may be sometimes asked to issue the medical certificate.

The deceased's possessions will have to be removed from the hospital, with a receipt needing to be signed on removal. If the medical certificate of the cause of death can be signed in the hospital then relatives will have to make arrangements to remove the body from the hospital mortuary. This will usually be the responsibility of the funeral director. Most funeral directors operate a 24-hour emergency service. However, there is no need to inform the director of a hospital death until the next morning after death. If cremation is involved, the necessary forms will be filled in at the hospital. The body cannot be removed until this is done. There will be a charge for filling in the forms.

Carrying out a post mortem in a hospital

A hospital will sometimes wish to carry out a post mortem, not involving the coroner. This cannot be carried out without the permission of the next of kin. In cases where a coroner is involved permission is not required. If a coroner orders a post mortem then this is legally required and cannot be prevented. Results are not automatically given to relatives and a request for these may have to be made.

The procedure for registering a death is the same as for a death outside a hospital. The registration however, must be within the district where the hospital is situated. Where there are no relatives or others to meet the cost of the funeral then the health authority has the power to do so. There are usually arrangements with local funeral directors to provide a simple funeral for the deceased.

The donation of organs for transplantation

Organ transplants help to save the lives of several thousand people per year and some thought needs to be given as to the possibility of donating organs from the dead person. Organs must be removed as soon as possible after death to prevent deterioration, which renders them useless. No organ can be removed for transplantation until a person is declared brain dead, known as "stem" death. In order to determine brain stem death a number of stringent tests are carried out, the criteria of which are laid down by the Royal College of Surgeons. A patient must be under 75 years of age for their major organs to be suitable for transplantation. The patient must be HIV negative and free from major infection. He or she must be of a compatible blood group to the planned recipient of the organs.

Organs that can be transplanted

Essentially, the organs intended for transplant must be in good order. For example, the lungs of a heavy smoker would be unsuitable. The following are the most commonly used for transplantation:

Heart

Heart transplants are considered for those patients with severe cardiac failure who are considered unsuitable for heart surgery.

Kidney

Kidneys are viable for around 48 hours following retrieval from the donor.

Liver

Liver transplants are required for patients with congenital malformation of the liver, hepatic failure, chronic liver disease, some cases of cancer and inborn metabolic errors.

Heart and lung

This particular operation is carried out for people with an advanced primary lung disease, or a condition leading to this, or lung disease arising as a result of cardiac problems.

The pancreas

Pancreas transplants are used for patients with type 1 diabetes. This operation may be solely a pancreas transplant or can be done together with the kidneys.

Lungs

One or both lungs can be transplanted.

Cornea

Damage to the cornea is a major cause of blindness. Cornea grafting is one major solution to blindness. There is no age limit for corneal donation and corneas can be removed up to 24 hours after the heart has stopped beating. Relatives of patients not dying in a hospital who want to carry out their wishes should first of all consult the donors GP or the ophthalmic department of the local hospital.

Heart valves

These can be transplanted following removal from a donor up to 72 hours after death.

There are other parts of the body, which can be transplanted including the skin, bone, connective tissue, major blood vessels, fettle cells and bone marrow.

When deciding whether or not to donate organs, religious and other cultural considerations will play a significant part. For Christians, organ donation is considered acceptable to Roman Catholics and Protestants. Christian Scientists, on the other hand, object to all forms of transplants. Buddhists do not object neither does the Jewish faith, with the exception of some orthodox Jews. Mormons have no objection neither do Hindu and Sikh. Muslims tend towards prohibition of organ transplants.

The National Health Service Organ Donor Register

This register is a computer data base set up at the UK transplant Support Service Authority (UKTSSA). All transplant coordinators have access to the register, and it can be checked each time a donor becomes available. Although relatives of donors are still asked for their permission to donate, the fact that details are on the register and there is a donor card carried, the decision is made easier by inclusion on the register.

Any driving licence issued after 1993 may be marked on the back indicating willingness to donate organs. Anyone wishing to be entered onto the register can do so by post or using a form available from doctor's surgeries, chemists, libraries and other public places.

157

Donation of a body for medical uses

Some people wish their body to used for medical education or research after death. If this was the wish of the deceased then the next of kin or the executor should contact HM Inspector of Anatomy for details of the relevant anatomy school. This should be done immediately after death. Offering a body may not lead to it being accepted due to too many offers or the nature of the death or whether the coroner is involved or how far away the body is.

Donation of the brain for medical research

Brain donation is a separate issue altogether from Organ donation and cannot be included on the NHS register. The Parkinson' Disease Society Brain Research Centre, which is part of the Institute of Neurology at the University College of London must be instructed to the effect that the donor wishes to donate the brain and potential donors must inform the society in advance or leave clear instructions that this should be done in the event of their death. It will be the responsibility of the medical school to make arrangements and pay for the funeral. The school will make arrangements for a simple funeral unless the relatives indicate otherwise.

Registration in Scotland

In Scotland the medical certificate of the cause of death is very similar to that in England. The obligation to give a certificate rests on the doctor who attended the dead person during their last illness. If there was no certificate in attendance then any doctor can issue a certificate. In most cases the certificate is given to a relative who will then send or give it to the Registrar of Deaths in their area. If a medical certificate of cause of death cannot be given, the registrar can register the death but must report the matter to the Procurator Fiscal.

There are no coroners as such in Scotland and the duties of a coroner are carried out by a Procurator fiscal. This particular person is a law officer and comes under the jurisdiction of the Lord Advocate. The key functions of the procurator fiscal includes responsibility for the investigation of all unexpected deaths including those under suspicious circumstances. If he or she is satisfied with the doctor's medical certificate and any police evidence then no further action will usually be taken. If there is doubt then a medical surgeon will be asked to report.

In most cases, a post mortem is not carried out and the doctor certifies the cause of death after an external examination. In those situations where a post mortem is deemed necessary then permission is sought from the sheriff. Where there is a possibility of criminal proceedings connected to the death then two surgeons will usually carry out the post mortem.

Death whilst in legal custody or at work must be the subject of a public enquiry which will take the place of an inquest in England. If the death is by natural causes, then there may not be a public enquiry.

A public enquiry is held before the sheriff in the local sheriff court. The procurator fiscal examines the witnesses but it is the sheriff who determines the cause of death. When the enquiry is completed the procurator fiscal notifies the result of the findings to the registrar general. If the death has not already been registered then the registrar general lets the local registrar in the district in which the death occurred know of the death.

In Scotland the law requires that every death must be registered within eight days of death. The person qualified to act as an informant is any relative of the dead person, any person present at the death, the deceased executor or other representative, the occupier of the premises where the death took place, or any person having knowledge of the particulars to be registered. The death may be registered in the office for the district in which the death occurred or in the office in the district where the deceased had resided before his or her death.

The death of anyone visiting Scotland must be registered where the death took place.

Registering a stillbirth

A stillbirth in Scotland must be registered within 21 days. A doctor or midwife will usually issue a certificate or the person informing can fill in a form 7, issued by the local registrar. In all cases of doubt, the Procurator Fiscal will get involved.

If the body is to be cremated then a certificate of stillbirth must be given by the doctor who was present at the confinement.

Death Certificates

As is the practice in England, the Registrar will issue free of charge a certificate of registration of death which can be used for National Insurance purposes. All other death certificates carry a fee.

A list of fees for the various functions carried out by the registrar can be obtained from any registrar's office, as in England.

Steps After Registration

If you need to make arrangements in relation to the dead person's estate then you will need to obtain several copies of the certified death certificate. The cost is minor, changing in April of every year. You will find that a separate certificate is needed for application for probate, for dealing with banks and insurance company's etc. Before applying for the death certificate then you should estimate how many you are likely to need.

It is important that you notify the benefits agency about the death as you will need to make arrangements about pensions etc. There may be a number of other benefits that you can claim after death, including help with funeral costs from the social fund. The funeral director may have a stock of the appropriate forms, which you must fill in.

In addition to copies of the death certificate, the registrar will provide another certificate, known as the green certificate to say that the death is now registered and a funeral can go ahead. The funeral director cannot proceed without it. If the coroner is or has been involved in the death then a different process takes place, which will be outlined a little later on.

If a registrars certificate has been issued before registration then the deceased can be buried only, if issued after registration then it can be cremated. The funeral director will forward the certificate either to the cemetery authority or to the vicar of the appropriate churchyard or to the office of the local crematorium. Copies of a death certificate can be obtained at a later date from the superintendent registrar if more than one month has elapsed or from the registrar if still relatively soon after the date of death.

Applications for certificates by post can be made to the general register office, see addresses at the rear of this book. In Northern Ireland it should be made to the Registrar General. There is a fee, again relatively minor and a stamped addressed envelope will be needed.

****

Ch. 12

The Law and Neighbours

The majority of people live peaceably with their neighbours. In fact, good relations with neighbours is essential for the maintenance of a healthy and balanced community. However, it is also the case that, at times, relations with neighbours break down and people turn to the law to obtain justice.

It is an unfortunate fact, particularly in the large urban centres, such as London, that people can live for years in a street and not know their neighbours. People become landlords and let their properties, which can lead to disruption if the incoming tenants are anti-social and do not have strong ties to an area.

The law strikes a balance when dealing with neighbour disputes. On one hand, people are free to use their property as they wish. On the other, it is essential that the rights of others are respected when we decide to embark on a course of action in our own property.

There are specialist organisations, based on mediation, who try to resolve disputes without recourse to the law. These organisations are usually within local authority areas, are free and can resolve disputes through mediating with the parties involved. See useful addresses for addresses of mediators.

In law, we both have a 'duty of care' and a duty to be reasonable to our neighbours. Essentially, this duty is to treat a person or people with the same degree of care and respect that we would expect to be afforded. It is when this is not the case that the law comes into play.

Neighbours and noise complaints

Of all the complaints that neighbours level against each other, the most common is that of noise. Noise can arise from many different sources, crying babies, footsteps and general movement, parties, dogs and so on. In each case, the law would recognise a reasonable level, over which legal action is seen to be reasonable. Generally, the local environmental health department of the council would provide measurements of noise and would determine what is reasonable. One main problem that has arisen is that of inadequate sound proofing, particularly in converted flats and new build properties. Builders have tended to construct properties with a minimum level of soundproofing that has proved to be inadequate.

In all disputes with neighbours, resorting to the law should be the last course of action. There are a number of other alternatives to consider first. It is always best to try to solve problems amicably. In the long run this proves the most fruitful as you will likely be neighbours for a long time to come and you will want to maintain good relationships.

The first thing to do is to talk to your neighbours and to establish what the nature of the problem is and whether your neighbours can acknowledge that there is a problem and do something about it. It might also help to speak to other neighbours and see whether they are also affected in the same way.

It is advisable to keep written records of the noise, a diary of sorts, recording the nature and type of noise and the frequency. This is the only way to create a tangible body of evidence.

Contacting landlords

If you feel that you cannot solve the problem by approaching the people concerned then it may be necessary to contact a landlord. The nature of a landlord can have a bearing on a person's ability to solve a case, whether the landlord is a social landlord, i.e. a housing association or local authority or private landlord. In many cases, the person creating the noise will also be an owner-occupier.

Social landlords

If the landlord of a person or people creating a noise is a social landlord, i.e. a housing association or local authority, the first thing that you should do, having tried to solve the problem amicably and started to keep a diary, is to contact the landlord and lodge a complaint, making it clear that you are maintaining a diary. The landlord will have signed a tenancy with the person involved and part of that tenancy agreement will be a covenant that the tenant does not cause a nuisance or annoyance to his/her neighbours. The landlord will contact the tenant and will begin the process whereby, ultimately; the tenant could be evicted for breach of tenancy.

However, it is important to realise that taking such action successfully can be a long and difficult process and it may be easier to take your own action, or at least take your own action in conjunction with the landlord.

Environmental Health Departments

The 1990 Environmental Protection Act (EPA) is the guiding framework within which environmental health officers operate. An individual can go direct to the Environmental Health Department, as can a landlord. In addition, the Environmental Health Department can also take action against individuals without waiting for a complaint to come in. To compliment environmental health, a landlord, particularly social landlords, can use independent witnesses to back up other bodies. Some local authorities operate 'noise patrols' which are intended to back up other evidence.

The EHO (Environmental Health Officer) will usually write a letter to the offending person, which will serve as a warning. If this does not work, then the EHO will write a letter stating that the individual is in breach of Section 80 of the EPA and, if the noise is not abated then the matter can become a criminal offence with a fine and/or prison sentence attached to it.

Using the Magistrates Court

There are other alternatives to the Environmental Health Department. A person suffering noise nuisance can go to the Magistrates court, under section 82 of the Environmental Protection Act 1990. Before you do so you have to give your neighbour formal written warning of your intention to take the matter to the magistrate's court, and this may well be sufficient to stop the noise. If it does not, then you have to fill in the appropriate forms, which can be obtained from the magistrates court, and make an appointment for a hearing. The court will need to be satisfied that a genuine noise nuisance exists and that you have made an effort to solve it directly with your neighbour.

If they are satisfied then they will issue a 'noise abatement order' and it becomes a criminal offence to breach this order.

Using the county court

Going to the county court is another alternative. You could begin a civil action in a county court to obtain an injunction to stop noise. The complaint must, however, be serious and the noise intolerable to obtain an injunction.

Injunctions are expensive and difficult to obtain and the burden of proof that much greater. If you are attempting to obtain an injunction then you will almost certainly need a solicitor.

Owner-occupiers and noise

If you own your own property and the person causing the nuisance is also an owner-occupier them you will not have a landlord to complain to, unless the person is a leaseholder. If the person is a leaseholder then you should establish who the freeholder is, i.e. who built and sold the property and insist that this person takes action under the lease. In addition to this, you should complain to the Environmental health officer of the Local

Authority or go to the magistrate's court in order to attempt to stop the noise.

If the person is a freeholder, and there is no landlord then you can only pursue the remedies described, i.e. EHO or magistrates court.

You could try contacting the police. However, unless the problem is domestic violence or some other criminal offence, the police are reluctant to get involved.

Other sources of noise

There are many sources of noise, in particular street noise, that cannot be pinpointed to a neighbour but nevertheless cause distress to others. One such source of noise is that of car alarms. In addition, builders and others operating in the streets can also cause noise nuisance. In order to combat the problems of street noise, a Noise and Statutory Nuisance Act came into effect in 1994 and extends the scope of the Environmental Protection Act 1990, so that street noise is also classified as a statutory nuisance.

The Act covers nuisance from vehicles, machinery or equipment in the street. It deals in particular with car alarms and burglar alarms. The concept of 'street' covers not only roads but also pathways, square or court open to the public. It does not mater whether the area is private or public. 'Equipment' includes musical equipment and even ice cream vans and buskers.

The exclusions

The Act does not apply to traffic noise, political demonstrations or noise made by any 'naval, military or air force'.

Car alarms

The person responsible for a car with a faulty alarm is the person who is the registered owner of the vehicle, or any other person who, for the time being, is responsible for the vehicle. An Environmental Health Officer can serve an abatement notice on that person to remedy the fault. The EHO can serve a notice on the vehicle and, if after an hour nothing further has been done or the person responsible has not been found, the EHO can either immobilise the alarm or remove the vehicle. The EHO has powers to open and enter a car, causing as little damage as possible. It must also be secured against theft when the EHO has completed the task.

House alarms

Householders have to inform local authorities of alarms that they intend to install. The alarm must meet prescribed requirements and the police must be informed of any key holders and of their telephone numbers. If any alarm is still operating one hour after it has been set off, then an officer of the local authority can enter and turn off that alarm providing that he or she has permission to do so. If no permission from the owner is forthcoming then a warrant can be obtained from a justice of the peace to enter the premises, if necessary by force, as long as damage is kept to a minimum and the premises is secured. The owner can be called upon to reimburse the authority for any cost incurred.

Problems with boundaries and fences

There is no absolute rule of law that requires a person to mark a boundary of his or her property or to enclose it with a fence. However, even if there are no rules, it is always advisable to reach agreement with neighbours about boundaries. If you are buying a property, always try to ensure that the boundaries are clearly marked and that it is clear what land you will own. Ascertain rights of way and car parking, if appropriate. Be very wary of buying a property where the plan does not tally with what you actually see on the ground. If in doubt contact the boundary skills panel of the Royal Institution of Chartered Surveyors (see useful addresses).

Plans

In general, with any conveyance of land there should be a plan. annexed to the title deeds, which is supposed to show where the boundaries to a property lie. However, a plan can be inaccurate, misleading or out of date. If you have not established the boundaries before you move in and trouble arises from a neighbour, the question is, what is the remedy?

The objective test

In general, the court will take an objective view, i.e. what are the facts? The court will look at the plan but will also look at all the surrounding circumstances that have resulted in the situation arising. On many occasions, there will be a trip arranged to the disputed are in order to ascertain the nature of the problem.

Fences

Even where there is no demarcation dispute between neighbours a frequent source of tension can be responsibility for the upkeep of fences. Who owns the fence and who should keep it in repair?

General rules regarding ownership

There are certain assumptions about responsibility for fences. Generally, where title deeds do have a plan then that plan will demark any fence ownership and if the 'T' mark used to demark the fence falls on your side then you will be responsible.

No 'T' marks or no plan

If there is no 'T'mark or no plan then there is a general assumption that you own the fence if the supporting posts are on your land.

Party fences

You can decide to have a party fence with both sides owning the fence and both sides contributing to the costs of repair. This is usually prevalent where ownership cannot be ascertained. Part wall legislation will generally find that both parties are responsible for the upkeep.

Mending fences

In general, if a fence belongs to a neighbour he or she is not under a legal duty to repair it. You can only insist on repair if it represents a hazard to your land and property. In this case, you can approach an environmental health officer and lodge a complaint under the Environmental Health Act. If you need to repair the fence at your own expense because it is a danger, you will need your neighbour's permission to go on to his/her land, otherwise you are trespassing. Otherwise, you would have to go to court for leave to go onto the land.

Party walls

In theory, a neighbour on each side of a party wall owns half the wall, whether the division is made vertically or horizontally. Where two buildings have been standing for 20 years or more, each neighbour acquires a right, called an easement, against the neighbour on the other side for the right of support to their property.

General duty to take care

It is reasonable for the law to impose a duty to take care on the owner of a party wall, so that whether he uses it, removes it, builds on it, or repairs it he must minimise the possibility of damage to neighbouring property. In addition, allowing a party wall to fall into disrepair can cause a nuisance and an adjoining owner can sue for damages.

Problems with nuisance generally

There are three types of nuisances, or categories of nuisance in law:

- private nuisance
- public nuisance
- statutory nuisance

Private nuisance

A private nuisance has been defined as something that occurs on someone else's property, which detrimentally affects your property or your enjoyment of your own property. Equally, something that happens on your property can be a source of nuisance to your neighbour. As we have discussed, the first course of action to be taken when dealing with private nuisance is that of approaching your neighbour and trying to find a remedy. Only then should there be recourse to the law. The Environmental Protection Act 1990 is the Act that regulates nuisance. However, with private nuisance, Environmental Health officers are reluctant to get involved unless the nuisance is prolonged and severe.

Public nuisance

A public nuisance is something that detrimentally affects a large group of people and not only an individual. It often concerns obstructions on the highways.

Statutory nuisance

Certain types of nuisance are covered by legislation. In particular, the Environmental protection Act 1990 has laid down various matters associated with property. As the name of the Act suggests, the law is primarily concerned with those who use their property in such a way as to cause a potential health hazard. The Act refers to the state of the premises, smoke, fumes, dust and any accumulation or deposit of substances that could be prejudicial to health or could cause a nuisance.

It is the well being of the population as a whole that the Act is concerned with. However, you can use its provisions for the protection of your own well being by notifying your local authority of apparent breaches.

The local authority has to take steps to remedy a breach, by investigating a complaint and warning a perpetrator if there is cause to do so. If the matter has to be taken further then the Act provides for a series of steps that ultimately lead to criminal action and a fine or imprisonment if found guilty.

Problems with gardens
Overhanging plants and trees
The general rule is that you are entitled to your own space, in and above (to some extent) your own property. So branches from neighbours trees or shrubs which overhang your garden are intrusions into your space, therefore they can be regarded as trespass and nuisance. You are entitled to lop off branches which intrude over your side of the fence. You are supposed to return the branches to your neighbour (and any growth such as fruit). However, in these cases, it is better to negotiate with your neighbour before taking action. If you need to gain access to someone else's property to deal with tress and shrubs then you have the right to apply to court under the Access to Neighbouring Land Act 1992 to allow you to solve the problem.

Obviously, this is extreme and is usually done where the landlord cannot be found or identified.

The same rules apply to roots that are growing into your property and are causing damage. You can cap those roots, as long as the tree is not damaged or you can apply to court for an injunction to prevent any further growth and also sue for damages.

Ch. 13

The Law and Landlord and Tenant

Explaining the law

As a landlord or tenant it is very important to understand rights and obligations, exactly what can and what cannot be done once the tenancy agreement has been signed and the tenant has moved into the property. Some landlords think they can do exactly as they please, because the property belongs to them. Some tenants do not know any differently and therefore the landlord can, and often does, get away with breaking the law. However, it is important that both landlord and tenants have a grasp on the key principles of the law.

In order to fully understand the law we should begin by looking at the main types of relationship between people and their homes.

The freehold and the lease

In law, there are two main types of ownership and occupation of property. These are: freehold and leasehold. These arrangements are very old indeed.

Freehold

If a person owns their property outright (usually with a mortgage) then they are a freeholder. The only claims to ownership over and above their own might be those of the building society or the bank, which lent them the money to buy the place. They will re-possess the property if the mortgage payments are not kept up with.

In certain situations though, the local authority (council) for an area can affect a person's right to do what they please with their home even if they are a freeholder. This will occur when planning powers are exercised, for example, in order to prevent the carrying out of alterations without consent.

The local authority for your area has many powers and we will be referring to these regularly in each Chapter of this Guide.

Leasehold

If a person lives in a property owned by someone else and has a written agreement allowing them to occupy the flat or house for a period of time i.e., giving them permission to live in that property, then they will, in the main, have a lease and either be a leaseholder or a tenant of a landlord.

The main principle of a lease is that a person has been given permission by someone else to live in his or her property for a period of time. The person giving permission could be either the freeholder or another leaseholder.

The tenancy agreement is one type of lease. If you have issued a tenancy agreement then you will have given permission to a person live in your property for a period of time.

The position of the tenant

The tenant will usually have an agreement for a shorter period of time than the typical leaseholder. Whereas the leaseholder will, for example, have an agreement for ninety-nine years, the tenant will have an agreement, which either runs from week to week or month to month (periodic tenancy) or is for a fixed term, for example, one-year.

These arrangements are the most common types of agreement between the private landlord and tenant. The agreement itself will state whether it is a fixed term or periodic tenancy. If an agreement has not been issued it will be assumed to be a periodic tenancy. Both periodic and fixed term tenants will usually pay a sum of rent regularly to a landlord in return for permission to live in the property.

The tenancy agreement

The tenancy agreement is the usual arrangement under which one person will live in a property owned by another. Before a tenant moves into a property he/she will have to sign a tenancy agreement drawn up by a landlord or landlord's agent.

A tenancy agreement is a contract between landlord and tenant.

It is important to realize that when you sign a tenancy agreement, you have signed a contract with another person, which governs the way in which they will live in their property.

The contract

Typically, any tenancy agreement will show the name and address of the landlord and will state the names of the tenant(s). The type of tenancy agreement that is signed should be clearly indicated. This could be, for example, a Rent Act protected tenancy, an assured tenancy or an assured shorthold tenancy. In the main, the agreement will be an assured shorthold.

The date the tenancy began and the duration (fixed term or periodic) plus the amount of rent payable should be clearly shown, along with who is responsible for any other charges, such as water rates, council tax etc, and a description of the property you are renting out.

In addition to the rent that must be paid there should be a clear vindication of when a rent increase can be expected. This information is sometimes shown in other conditions of tenancy, which should be given to the tenant when they move into their home. The conditions of tenancy will set out landlords and tenants rights and obligations.

If services are provided, i.e., if a service charge is payable, this should be indicated in the agreement. The tenancy agreement should indicate clearly the address to which notices on the landlord can be served by the tenant, for example, because of repair problems or notice of leaving the property. The landlord has a legal requirement to indicate this.

174

The tenancy agreement will either be a basic document with the above information or will be more comprehensive. Either way, there will be a section beginning "the tenant agrees." Here the tenant will agree to move into the property, pay rent, use the property as an only home, not cause a nuisance to others, take responsibility for certain internal repairs, not sublet the property, i.e., create another tenancy, and various other things depending on the property.

There should also be another section "the landlord agrees". Here, the landlord is contracting with the tenant to allow quiet enjoyment of the property. The landlord's repairing responsibilities are also usually outlined.

Finally, there should be a section entitled "ending the tenancy" which will outline the ways in which landlord and tenant can end the agreement. It is in this section that the landlord should make reference to the "grounds for possession". Grounds for possession are circumstances where the landlord will apply to court for possession of his/her property. Some of these grounds relate to what is in the tenancy, i.e., the responsibility to pay rent and to not cause a nuisance.

Other grounds do not relate to the contents of the tenancy directly, but more to the law governing that particular tenancy. The grounds for possession are very important, as they are used in any court case brought against the tenant. Unfortunately, they are not always indicated in the tenancy agreement. As they are so important they are summarized later on in this chapter.

It must be said at this point that many residential tenancies are very light on landlord's responsibilities. Repairing responsibilities, and responsibilities relating to rental payment, are landlords obligations under law. This book deals with these, and other areas. However, many landlords will seek to use only the most basic document in order to conceal legal obligations.

The public sector tenancy (local authority or housing association), for example, is usually very clear and very comprehensive about the rights and obligations of landlord and tenant. Unfortunately, the private landlord often does not employ the same energy when it comes to educating and informing the tenant. This is one of the main reasons for this book. It is essential that those who intend to let property for profit are able to manage professionally and set high standards as a private landlord. This is because the sector has been beset by rogues in the past.

Different types of tenancy agreement
The Protected tenancy - the meaning of the term

As a basic guide, if a person is a private tenant and signed their current agreement with a landlord before 15th January 1989 then they will, in most cases, be a protected tenant with all the rights relating to protection of tenure, which are considerable. Protection is provided under the 1977 Rent Act.

In practice, there are not many protected tenancies left and the investor will usually be managing an assured shorthold tenancy.

The Assured shorthold tenancy - what it means

If the tenant entered into an agreement with a landlord after 15th January 1989 then they will, in most cases, be an assured tenant. We will discuss assured tenancies in more depth in chapter seven. In brief, there are various types of assured tenancy. The assured shorthold is usually a fixed term version of the assured tenancy and enables the landlord to recover their property after six months and to vary the rent after this time.

At this point it is important to understand that the main difference between the two types of tenancy, protected and assured, is that the tenant has less rights as a tenant under the assured tenancy. For example, they will not be entitled, as is a protected tenant, to a fair rent set by a Rent Officer.

Other types of agreement

In addition to the above tenancy agreements, there are other types of agreement sometimes used in privately rented property. One of these is the company let and another is the license agreement. The person signing such an agreement is called a licensee.

Licenses will only apply in special circumstances where the licensee cannot be given sole occupation of his home and therefore can only stay for a short period with minimum rights. It is not the intention to pursue licensees further in this book.

Squatting

From September 1st 2012, squatting in a residential property became a criminal offence. Squatters can now be arrested and if convicted, can be sent to prison for up to 6 months or fined up to £5,000, or both.

What is squatting?

Squatting is when somebody enters and lives in a property or on land without the permission of the owner or the person legally entitled to occupy it (for example, a tenant). Squatting isn't a legal term, but is commonly used to describe a trespasser who has entered and lives in a property without the permission of the owner or another person legally entitled to occupy it. Former tenants and licensees who stay on in a property after their tenancy or licence has ended may be trespassers, but are not squatters because they originally had the right or permission to enter the property. More information on squatting is available from the Advisory Service for Squatters.

The criminal law on squatting

Squatting in a residential property is a criminal offence. Squatters can be arrested by the police and if convicted by a court, can be sent to prison for up to 6 months, fined up to £5,000, or both. You cannot be convicted of squatting if you:

- are squatting in commercial premises
- are a tenant or licensee remaining in a property after the tenancy or licence has ended
- entered the property genuinely believing you were a tenant – for example, if a bogus letting agent rented you a property they had no right to
- are a Gypsy or Traveller living on an unauthorised site.

It is illegal to get into a property by breaking in or damaging windows and doors and you could be arrested even if the damage is minimal.

Squatters have a right to be connected to utilities such as gas, electricity and water, but using them without contacting the supplier first is illegal.

How squatters can be evicted

Even if they are not arrested, squatters can be evicted more easily than many other people. In some cases the person with a right to occupy or live in the property doesn't have to get a court order first – this applies if you are:

- squatting in a property and excluding somebody from their home (a 'displaced residential occupier') – for example, if they were on holiday
- squatting in a property that somebody is about to move into (a 'protected intending occupier'), such as a homebuyer or a new tenant.

In most cases the court will automatically give the owner or landlord the right to get back into the property. If you still don't leave, they can also ask the court bailiffs to evict you and your belongings from the property.

It is illegal to use violence to evict squatters

It is illegal for the owner or landlord to use or threaten you with violence. This is the case even if the owner or landlord has a court order to evict you.

It is illegal for an owner, landlord or tenant to use force, such as breaking down the door, to get into the property while you or another squatter are inside, unless they are a 'displaced residential occupier' or a 'protected intending occupier'.

-The tenancy or the contract was entered into before 15th January 1989;

Security of tenure: The ways in which a tenant can lose their home as an assured shorthold tenant

There are a number of circumstances called grounds (mandatory and discretionary) whereby a landlord can start a court action to evict a tenant.

These are *mandatory* grounds (where the judge must give the landlord possession) and *discretionary* grounds (where the judge does not have to give the landlord possession) on which a court can order possession if the home is subject to an assured tenancy. The grounds cover such things as non-payment of rent and nuisance. A full copy of the grounds can be found in the 1988 Housing Act. A copy can be obtained from your local library, or a digest of the grounds can be found on the internet.

Fast track possession

In November 1993, following changes to the County Court Rules, a facility was introduced which enables landlords of tenants with assured shorthold tenancies to apply for possession of their property without the usual time delay involved in waiting for a court date and attendance at court. This is known as "fast track possession" It cannot be used for rent arrears or other grounds. It is used to gain possession of a property when the fixed term of six months or more has come to an end and the tenant will not move.

If the landlord wishes to raise rent, at least one month's minimum notice must be given. The rent cannot be raised more than once for the same tenant in one year. Tenants have the right to challenge a rent increase if they think it is unfair by referring the rent to a Rent Assessment Committee. The committee will prevent the landlord from raising the rent above the ordinary market rent for that type of property.

Joint Tenancies

Joint tenancies: the position of two or more people who have a tenancy agreement for one property. Although it is the normal state of affairs for a tenancy agreement, to be granted to one person, this is not always the case.

A tenancy can also be granted to two or more people and is then known as a *joint tenancy*. The position of joint tenants is exactly the same as that of single tenants. In other words, there is still one tenancy even though it is shared.

Each tenant is responsible for paying the rent and observing the terms and conditions of the tenancy agreement. No one joint tenant can prevent another joint tenants access to the premises.

If one of the joint tenants dies then his or her interest will automatically pass to the remaining joint tenants. A joint tenant cannot dispose of his or her interest in a will.

If one joint tenant, however, serves a notice to quit (notice to leave the property) on another joint tenant(s) then the tenancy will come to an end and the landlord can apply to court for a possession order, if the remaining tenant does not leave.

The position of a wife or husband in relation to joint tenancies is rather more complex because the married person has more rights when it comes to the home than the single person.

Remember: the position of a tenant who has signed a joint tenancy

180

agreement is exactly the same as that of the single tenant. If one person leaves, the other(s) have the responsibilities of the tenancy. If one person leaves without paying his share of the rent then the other tenants will have to pay instead.

Rent
Rent control for assured shorthold tenants
We have seen that the assured shorthold tenancy is for a period of six months minimum. Like the assured tenant, the assured shorthold tenant has no right to request that a fair rent should be set. The rent is a market rent.

As with an assured tenancy, the assured shorthold tenant has the right to appeal to a Rent Assessment Committee in the case of what he/she considers an unreasonable rent. This may be done during the contractual term of the tenancy. The Committee will consider whether the rent is significantly higher than is usual for a similar property.

If the Committee assess a different rent from that set by the landlord, they may set a date when the increase will take effect. The rent cannot be backdated to before the date of the application. Once a decision has been reached by the Committee, the landlord cannot increase the rent for at least twelve months, or on termination of the tenancy.

Council tax and the tenant
Council tax is based on properties, or dwellings, and not individual people. This means that there is one bill for each individual dwelling, rather than separate bills for each person. The number and type of people who live in the dwelling may affect the size of the final bill. A discount of 25% is given for people who live alone. Each property is placed in a valuation band with different properties paying more or less depending on their individual value. Tenants who feel that their home has been placed in the wrong valuation band can appeal to their local authority council tax department.

Who has to pay the council tax?

In most cases the tenant occupying the dwelling will have to pay the council tax. However, a landlord will be responsible for paying the council tax where there are several households living in one dwelling. This will usually be hostels, bedsits and other non-self contained flats where people share things such as cooking and washing facilities. The council tax on this type of property remains the responsibility of the landlord even if all but one of the tenants move out. Although the landlord has the responsibility for paying the council tax, he or she will normally try to pass on the increased cost through rents. However, there is a set procedure for a landlord to follow if he/she wishes to increase rent.

Dwellings, which are exempt

Certain properties will be exempt from the council tax, such as student's halls of residences and nurse's homes. Properties with all students resident will be exempt from the tax. However, if one non-student moves in then that property will no longer be exempt from tax. Uninhabitable empty properties are exempt from tax, as they are not counted as dwellings. This is not the same as homes, which have been declared as unfit for human habitation by Environmental Health officers.

The deciding factor will be whether or not a property is capable of being lived in.

Benefits available for those on low income

Tenants on very low income, except for students, will usually be able to claim help with council tax . This will cover some of the council tax.

Tenants with disabilities may be entitled to further discounts. Tenants who are not responsible for individual council tax, but pay it through their rent, can claim housing benefit to cover the increase.

The rules covering council tax liability can be obtained from a Citizens Advice Bureau or from your local authority council tax department.

Deposits

A landlord can charge a *deposit*, to set against the possibility that a tenant may damage the property or furniture. For most types of tenancy the law puts a limit on the amount that can be charged. The normal amount is 1 month's rent. The deposit must be sent to one of several deposit schemes which came into existence after April 2007.

The right to quiet enjoyment of a home

Earlier, we saw that when a tenancy agreement is signed, the landlord is contracting to give quiet enjoyment of the tenants home. This means that they have the right to live peacefully in the home without harassment.

The landlord is obliged not to do anything that will disturb the right to the quiet enjoyment of the home. The most serious breach of this right would be for the landlord to wrongfully evict a tenant.

What can be done against unlawful evictions?

There are two main remedies for unlawful eviction: damages and, as stated above, an injunction.

The injunction

An injunction is an order from the court requiring a person to do, or not to do something. In the case of eviction the court can grant an injunction requiring the landlord to allow a tenant back into occupation of the premises. In the case of harassment an order can be made preventing the landlord from harassing the tenant. Failure to comply with an injunction is contempt of court and can result in a fine or imprisonment.

Damages

In some cases the tenant can press for *financial compensation* following unlawful eviction. Financial compensation may have to be paid in cases where financial loss has occurred or in cases where personal hardship alone has occurred. The tenant can also press for *special damages,* which means that the tenant may recover the definable out-of-pocket expenses. These could be expenses arising as a result of having to stay in a hotel because of the eviction. Receipts must be kept in that case. There are also *general damages,* which can be awarded in compensation for stress, suffering and inconvenience.

A tenant may also seek *exemplary damages* where it can be proved that the landlord has disregarded the law deliberately with the intention of making a profit out of the displacement of the tenant.

Repairs and improvements

Repairs and improvements generally: the landlord and tenants obligations

Repairs are essential works to keep the property in good order. Improvements are alterations to the property, e.g. the installation of a shower.

As we have seen, most tenancies are periodic, i.e. week-to-week or month-to-month. If a tenancy falls into this category, or is a fixed-term tenancy for less than seven years, and began after October1961, then a landlord is legally responsible for most major repairs to the flat or house.

If a tenancy began after 15th January 1989 then, in addition to the above responsibility, the landlord is also responsible for repairs to common parts and service fittings.

The area of law dealing with the landlord and tenants repairing obligations is the 1985 Landlord and Tenant Act, section 11.

This section of the Act is known as a covenant and cannot be excluded by informal agreement between landlord and tenant. In other words the landlord is legally responsible whether he or she likes it or not. Parties to a tenancy, however, may make an application to a court mutually to vary or exclude this section.

An example of repairs a landlord is responsible for:

Leaking roofs and guttering;
Rotting windows;
Rising damp;
Damp walls;
Faulty electrical wiring;
Dangerous ceilings and staircases;
Faulty gas and water pipes;
Broken water heaters and boilers;
Broken lavatories, sinks or baths.

In shared housing the landlord must see that shared halls, stairways, kitchens and bathrooms are maintained and kept clean and lit.

Normally, tenants are responsible only for minor repairs, e.g., broken door handles, cupboard doors, etc. Tenants will also be responsible for decorations unless they have been damaged as a result of the landlord's failure to do repair.

A landlord will be responsible for repairs only if the repair has been reported. It is therefore important to report repairs in writing and keep a copy. If the repair is not carried out then action can be taken. Damages can also be claimed.

Compensation can be claimed, with the appropriate amount being the reduction in the value of the premises to the tenant caused by the landlord's failure to repair. If the tenant carries out the repairs then the amount expended will represent the decrease in value.

The tenant does not have the right to withhold rent because of a breach of repairing covenant by the landlord. However, depending on the repair, the landlord will not have a very strong case in court if rent is withheld.

Reporting repairs to a landlord

The tenant has to tell the landlord or the person collecting the rent straight away when a repair needs doing. It is advisable that it is in writing, listing the repairs that need to be done. Once a tenant has reported a repair the landlord must do it within a reasonable period of time. What is reasonable will depend on the nature of the repair. If certain emergency work needs to be done by the council, such as leaking guttering or drains a notice can be served ordering the landlord to do the work within a short time. In exceptional cases if a home cannot be made habitable at reasonable cost the council may declare that the house must no longer be used, in which case the council has a legal duty to rehouse a tenant.

If after the council has served notice the landlord still does not do the work, the council can send in its own builder or, in some cases take the landlord to court. A tenant must allow a landlord access to do repairs. The landlord has to give twenty-four hours notice of wishing to gain access.

Can the landlord put the rent up after doing repairs?

If there is a service charge for maintenance, the landlord may be able to pass on the cost of the work(s).

Tenants rights to make improvements to a property

Unlike carrying out repairs the tenant will not normally have the right to insist that the landlord make actual alterations to the home. However, a tenant needs the following amenities and the law states that you should have them:

Bath or shower;
Wash hand basin;
Hot and cold water at each bath, basin or shower;
An indoor toilet.

If these amenities do not exist then the tenant can contact the council's Environmental Health Officer. An improvement notice can be served on the landlord ordering him to put the amenity in.

Disabled tenants

If a tenant is disabled he/she may need special items of equipment in the accommodation. The local authority may help in providing and, occasionally, paying for these. The tenant will need to obtain the permission of the landlord. If you require more information then contact the social services department locally.

Shared housing. The position of tenants in shared houses (Houses in Multiple Occupation)

The law lays down special standards for shared housing (houses in multiple occupation). Local authorities have special powers to deal with bad conditions when they occur. The legal regulations for houses in multiple occupation are set out in the Housing (Management of Houses in Multiple Occupation) Regulations 1990 and also the Housing Act 2005. There is now a licensing scheme in place where a landlord of a HMO has to apply for a licence annually and submit to inspections.

The manager of a house in multiple occupation has responsibilities under the management regulations to carry out repair, maintenance and cleaning work and also safety work necessary to protect residents from risk of injury. A notice must be displayed where all the residents can see it showing the name, address and telephone number of the manager. Landlords must ensure that main entrances shared passageways, staircases and other common areas are maintained. All services such as gas, electricity and water supplies, plus drainage facilities, must also be maintained. The same rules apply to the internal areas of living accommodation. In addition, there is a duty to maintain adequate fire safety, as obviously, shared housing is at greater risk of fire. Self-closing fire doors, emergency escape lighting, fire alarms and detectors and fire fighting equipment will normally be required.

Signs indicating fire escape routes must be displayed where they are easy to see.

There are also rules concerning overcrowding in shared housing. The local authority has powers to tackle overcrowding problems; landlords, on request, have to supply the local authority with numbers of individuals and households in a shared house. Tenants also have duties, which enable landlords to fulfill their legal responsibilities. Tenants should allow landlords access at reasonable times, give details of all who live in the accommodation, and take care to avoid damage to property.

Going to court to regain possession of a home

There may come a time when you need to go to court to regain possession of your property. This will usually arise when the contract has been breached by the tenant, for non-payment of rent or for some other breach such as nuisance or harassment. As we have seen, a tenancy can be brought to an end in a court on one of the grounds for possession. However, as the tenancy will usually be an assured shorthold then it is necessary to consider whether you are in a position to give two months notice and withhold the deposit, as opposed to going to court.

If you decide, for whatever reason, to go to court, then any move to regain your property for breach of agreement will commence in the county court in the area in which the property is. The first steps in ending the tenancy will necessitate the serving of a notice of seeking possession using one of the Grounds for Possession detailed earlier in the book. If the tenancy is protected then 28 days must be given, the notice must be in prescribed form and served on the tenant personally (preferably).

If the tenancy is assured shorthold, which is more often the case now, then 14 days notice of seeking possession can be used. In all cases the ground to be relied upon must be clearly outlined in the notice.

If the case is more complex, then this will entail a particulars of claim being prepared, usually by a solicitor, as opposed to a standard possession form.

A fee is paid when sending the particulars and summons to court. Both of these forms can be obtained from the court. When completed, the forms should be sent in duplicate to the county court and a copy retained for you. The court will send a copy of the Particulars of claim and the summons to the tenant. They will send you a form which gives you a case number and court date to appear, known as the return date.

On the return date, you should arrive at court at least 15 minutes early. You can represent yourself in simple cases but are advised to use a solicitor for more contentious cases. When it is your turn to present the case, you should have your file in order, a copy of all relevant notices served and a current rent arrears figure or a copy of the particulars for other cases.

If it is simple rent arrears then quite often the judge will guide you through. However, the following are the steps to observe:

-State your name and address
-Tenants name and address
-Start date of tenancy
-Current rent and arrears
-Date notice served-a copy should be produced for the judge
-Circumstances of tenant (financial and other) this is where you
  make your case
-Copy of order wanted

If the tenant is present then they will have a chance to defend themselves. A number of orders are available. However, if you have gone to court on the mandatory ground eight then if the fact is proved then you will get possession immediately. If not, then the judge can grant an order, suspended whilst the tenant finds time to pay.

In a lot of cases, it is more expedient for a landlord to serve notice-requiring possession, if the tenancy has reached the end of the period, and then wait two months before the property is regained. This saves the cost and time of going to court particularly if the ground is one of nuisance or other, which will involve solicitors. In many cases, if you are contemplating going to court and have never been before and do not know the procedure then it is best to use a solicitor to guide the case through. Costs can be recovered from the tenant, although this depends on the tenant's means.

If you regain possession of your property midway through the contractual term then you will have to complete the possession process by use of bailiff, a fee of £150 (approx) and another form, Warrant for Possession of Land used. (check fees with the county court in your area)

If you have reached the end of the contractual term and wish to recover your property then a "fast track" procedure is available which entails gaining an order for possession and bailiff's order by post. This can be used in cases with the exception of rent arrears.

****

Ch. 14

The Police-Getting Arrested-Making a Complaint Against the Police

There are many reasons why the police might arrest a citizen, a few of those are:

- Driving offences
- Burglary
- Carrying offensive weapons
- Fighting
- Drink and drugs

If the police suspect that you are carrying offensive weapons or other illegal items or substances, they can stop and search without a warrant. If this happens then you can ask to see identification and you have the right to ask why you are being stopped and searched. The police do not have the right to intimidate or bully you.

Search of premises or home

The police have powers to search a premises or a home if they feel that evidence against you found there can help them with their enquiries. They can search a premise's with the consent of an occupier, or a warrant can be obtained from a magistrate to further their enquiries. They can search any premises without a warrant on a number of occasions such as:

- To capture an escaped prisoner

191

- To protect life or to stop serious damage to property
- Arrest someone for an arrestable offence or public disorder offence
- After an arrest to search a detained persons premises

Many other laws give police powers to enter premises, i.e. terrorism, harbouring an escaped convict and so on. Someone is allowed to be present when the search is taking place unless they might hinder the investigation. The police should give information about their powers to search premises. They are not allowed to use unreasonable force and a record must be kept of the search..

You have no legal obligation or duty to help the police with their enquiries. The only way the police can force you to accompany them to the police station is to arrest you. The police can arrest a suspect by obtaining an arrest warrant from a magistrate. The magistrate will need to be convinced that there is a case against a suspect.

Police also have powers of arrest without a warrant in the following circumstances:

- An arrestable offence (one carrying a potential five-year sentence) has or could have been committed
- Certain other sp
- ecific offences have been committed such as rape, car theft, shoplifting or other theft offences
- If you are drunk or fail a breath test
- If you are soliciting or living off immoral earnings
- If you refuse to give details of your name and address if a particular law requires you to do so
- Where a breach of the peace has occurred or may occur.

What to do if you are arrested

It may be possible to avoid being arrested if you co-operate with the police in the first instance. However, if you are arrested, then you should be informed of your right to see a solicitor. It does not matter what time you are arrested, the duty solicitor scheme will mean that a solicitor will be on call and will speak to you over the telephone or come out to see you.

You should also be told that you have the right to inform some other person of your arrest. You should be told that you have a right to see the codes of practice followed by the police. You should be given a written note of the three rights above, which will contain the usual caution: '*You do not have to say anything, but it may harm your defence if you do not mention when questioned something which you later rely on in court. Anything you do say may be given in evidence*'.

This caution means that you have the right of silence. You do not have to say anything, in particular until a solicitor arrives. In very limited cases, the right of silence has been removed. What you say can be used in any legal proceedings that are brought against you.

It is generally wise to say nothing until a solicitor arrives and then the interview can be guided professionally. What you do say is tape-recorded.

Detaining suspects

If you have not been arrested then the police cannot keep you at the police station. When you have been arrested you should be charged with an offence within 24 hours (usually) or released. You can be held up to 36 hours for a serious offence. If the police wish to detain you for longer than this then they can apply to a magistrate's court for permission to do so. 96 hours is usually the maximum amount of time. The Police and Criminal Evidence Act (PACE) deals with rights when arrested.

Assuming that you have been charged with an offence then you will already have seen a solicitor. If you have not seen a solicitor then it is very wise to do so as they can guide you through the procedure and ensure that what takes place is fair.

After you have been charged, you will either be remanded in custody or let out on bail. If you are remanded in custody you will not be released until after the trial. Bail applications are not, or should not, be refused unnecessarily. However, you may have to provide sureties and comply with certain conditions such as reporting to the police station.

More minor offences are tried in the magistrate's court and more serious offences in the Crown Court. (See previous chapters).

You will need to prepare your case with your solicitor for the trial. There may be witnesses to locate and also statements to prepare. At the trial, you will either be found guilty or not guilty. If you are found not guilty there may be grounds for you to bring proceedings against the police for false imprisonment arising from your original arrest. If you are found guilty then you will be sentenced and at this stage any previous convictions are brought to light.

Once you have been convicted, you will have a criminal record. Some offences are so minor and commonplace that they are unlikely to affect your future employment or well being generally. However, more serious offences can have a serious effect and you should certainly take professional advice. Criminal records arising from different types of crime will last for different periods of time.

Making a complaint against the police

The Independent Police Complaints Commission (IPCC) supervises investigations into complaints against the police. As a member of the public, you can make complaints about the conduct of a police officer towards yourself if you think that you have good reason. You can also complain on someone else's behalf if you have their written authorisation.

The IPCC is an independent body set up by the government to oversee public complaints against police officers in the 43 police services in

England and Wales, plus the British Transport Police, Ministry of Defence, Port of Liverpool, Port of Tilbury, Royal parks and UKAEA police. The IPCC can investigate complaints direct from the public or referred directly from the police services.

If you do decide to make your complaint through the IPCC, send the details to the following address, making sure that all the relevant information is included:

Independent Police Complaints Commission
PO Box 473
Sale
M33 OBW
General Enquiries 0300 020 0096

****

INDEX

****

Useful Addresses

The Legal system

The Free Representation Unit
60 Greys Inn Road
London WC1X 8LU
020 7611 9555
www.fru.org.uk

The Law Society
020 7320 5650
www.lawsociety.org.uk

Legal Action Group
National Pro Bono Centre
48 Chancery Lane
London
WC2 1JF
020 7833 2931
http://www.lag.org.uk/

National Association of Citizens Advice bureau
3rd Floor North
200 Aldersgate street
London EC1A 4HD
0844 111 444
http://www.citizensadvice.org.uk/

Solicitors Regulation Authority
The Cube
199 Wharfeside Street
Birmingham

B1 1RN
0370 606 2555
www.sra.org.uk

Law and the Consumer

Advertising Standards Authority
Mid City Place
71 High Holborn
London WC1V 6QT
020 7492 2222
http://www.asa.org.uk

Association of British Travel Agents
30 Park Street
London SE1 9EQ
020 3117 0599
www.abta.com

Consumers Association
2 Marylebone Road
London NW1 4DF
01992 822 800
www.which.co.uk

Consumer Credit Association (UK)
1 Minerva Court
Minerva Avenue
Chester
CH1 4QT
Telephone: 01244 394760

Direct Marketing Association
DMA House
70 Margaret Street
London W1W 8SS
020 7291 3300
www.thedma.org

Direct Selling Association
Enterprise House
30 Billing Road
Northampton
NN1 5DQ
01604 625700
http://www.dsa.org.uk/

Children and the Law
Childline
NSPCC
Weston House
42 Curtain Road
London EC2A 3NH
www.childline.org
0800 800 5000 (adults)
0800 1111 (children and young people)

Child Support Solutions
152 Grove Lane
Timperley
Altrincham
Cheshire
WA15 6PD
03456 588683
www.childsupportsolutions.co.uk

The Children's Society
Edward Rudolf House
Margery Street
London WC1X OJL
0300 303 7000
http://www.childrenssociety.org.uk/

Divorce
Relate
0330 100 1234
www.relate.org.uk

Bereavement
Age UK
England
Tavis House 1-6 Tavistock Square
London WC1H 9NA
Tel: 0800 169 2081
www.ageuk.org.uk

Asian Funeral Service
www.asianfuneral.org

Association of Burial Authorities
www.cpalc.org.uk

British Organ Donors Society (Body)
Balsham,
Cambridge CB1 6DL
Tel/Fax 01223 893636
http://body.orpheusweb.co.uk/

Cremation Society
2nd Floor, Brecon House
16-16a Albion Place
Maidstone ME14 5DZ
Tel: 01622 688292/3
Fax: 01622 686698
www.cremation.co.uk

Cruse-Bereavement Care
PO Box 800
Richmond, TW9 1RG
Tel: 0208 939 9530
www.cruse.org.org. uk

The Lullaby Trust (Formerly Foundation for the Study of Infant Death)
11 Belgrave street
London SW1V 1RB
Tel: 0808 802 6868 (Helpline)
http://fsid.org.uk

****